Schizencephaly: Angels with Broken Wings

TRICIA DENNIS

and

STEPHANIE ZIEMANN

DEDICATION

Schizencephaly Awareness

In loving memory of

Jennifer Toby, Mariah Penrod,

and

Garrett Hudson

CONTENTS

What is Schizencephaly?

Schizencephaly is a very rare brain malformation that affects approximately 1 in 100,000 pregnancies, making it one of the most rare cephalic disorders. The causes are unknown, but may be linked to in-utero stroke, genetics, and even environmental issues; none of which have been confirmed. Doctors feel the migration of stem cells is disrupted between 4 to 9 weeks gestation, causing the cells to not form the brain properly. This disruption causes clefts, or missing areas of the brain.

There are two types of this disorder, Unilateral and Bilateral. Unilateral is defined with only one side of the brain being affected. Bilateral means both sides have clefts or missing areas.

Unilateral Schizencephaly is more mild than Bilateral Schizencephaly, but it still involves high or low tone, and in most cases, seizures. Unilateral children may have some developmental delays and speech impairment, but live fairly normal healthy lives and are often mainstreamed in school.

Bilateral Schizencephaly is more severe since it affects both sides of the brain. Most children do not live as long and have many more physical issues such as severe motor delays, little to no speech, paralysis to some degree on one or both sides of the body, seizures, and multiple surgeries throughout life to help with muscle spasms and various other complications.

Schizencephaly is a disorder with many issues attached to it. Many children will experience moderate to crippling scoliosis, difficulties with their bone structure, Epilepsy, Cerebral Palsy, poor vision or blindness, Microcephaly (small head), Hydrocephaly (water on the brain), seizures, and will need multiple therapies all through life to help the child or adult live.

The degree of damage, and whether the clefts are connected (Closed-Lip) or unconnected (Open-Lip), also plays a critical role in the development of people with this disorder. The deeper and wider the clefts, the more difficult seizures can be to control. In some cases, the seizures are uncontrollable and surgery is needed to either implant devices to help gain control, or doctors will remove portions of the damaged areas of the brain in an attempt to alleviate the person of seizures. Almost all children will present some seizure activity at some point with this disorder, and many will rely on medications to control them indefinitely.

Although technology and therapy has come a long way in the last 20 years, this disorder still remains a mystery. There are not enough resources or help available for families that get this diagnosis. With the help of the internet, people are able to find support and information, but are still seeking answers that are just not available.

This book was written to help educate and support families dealing with this disorder so we can learn from each other and seek answers from others facing this mystery called Schizencephaly.

These are our stories....

Noah

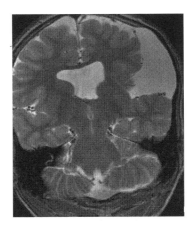

This is the story of my son, Noah. When he was born my mother called him her angel with a broken wing. Since then, hundreds of families have embraced this name to all of our children with Schizencephaly.

It was November 7, 2000, and I was now five months pregnant with my second child. Although it was not planned, I was just as excited. I was no pro to pregnancy, but I knew something was different. And being an American Indian, I was taught to go with my gut. This feeling was one that was there the entire first few months, and it was becoming a strong fear by now. My doctor insisted I was working myself up (a term I've since grown to hate), but in my heart, and even as a child, I had prepared myself for something big. I had no idea what until this day in and this month.

I can clearly remember being six years old and telling my mom and dad that one day I would a have sick child. They thought I had an active imagination, as I was always creating some skit for the family or putting drama into everything possible. But I knew, I always knew. I went against the doctor's orders after repeatedly telling him I felt this child tensing up inside me. My belly would become stiff and then little movement, then suddenly it would feel like the baby would ease up, still with little movement. I made my husband take me to the ER, where I lied and said I was having serious pain to get a second ultrasound. And it worked.

Pleased with myself, I sat in the dark room, my husband across, and my oldest son, River (age two at the time), in his lap. The tech began the ultrasound process with a smile on her face, excited to be the one to tell me the sex of the baby.

The first words I remember hearing were "It's a boy!" My husband and son both smiled as I watched her continue to look at my baby. I realized within seconds she was focused on the head and seemed to continuously push my stomach more to get a good look. I glanced at my husband and a tear fell down my face as he said, "Tricia, what is wrong?" I couldn't answer, but I knew the four minutes we spent looking at my baby's brain was exactly what I had been preparing my entire life for.

The nurse went to stand up and bumped the back of the machine, stating she was going to have the doctor come to explain how the baby was doing. I didn't even know if this child was alive at that point. Two minutes I sat with tears rolling down my face. It wouldn't stop. My husband kept telling me nothing was wrong, and I kept saying "This is bad." I was right.

The door swung open, and words that I will never forget came spewing out of his mouth like he was so detached from me that my feelings did not matter. "Your child has a disorder called

Schizencephaly. He is missing part of his brain, and we are sending you to counseling now." The door shut and I watched my husband drop his head. That was the first time I ever saw him cry.

We were whisked into a room with a man at a desk. All I heard was mumbling, but I did hear a few things such as, "Rare... seizures... grotesque... morbid." I kept focusing on the sign on the door. I did not hear anything, I was too busy thinking these people had no clue what was going on and I needed to get to a library immediately. Two words did stand out, mentally retarded. Those were the ones I remember hearing very clearly. I sat there looking at a paragraph long explanation, and I didn't even understand the words on the paper. I did know that this child would be named Noah, and he and I were about to begin a very long journey.

It was my mother's Birthday, and she had been preparing to head to dinner with friends when I knocked on her door and fell onto the stoop in tears. It finally hit me; I may never even get the chance to hold this little angel. Prior to that day, she and I never seemed to get along. It seems like no matter how awful the relationship, you always want your mom and dad whenever something happens. She immediately began asking me questions with her friends all huddled around. All I wanted was to stop and breathe, and to hug my father.

My father, being the quiet, humble man he was, had little words to say in life and a heart of gold. I wanted him desperately, but sadly he was working as usual. I lost it again when he picked up the phone, and between my sobbing I managed to get out the words, "Something is wrong with the baby." There was a long pause, and then I told him between tears it appeared the baby was damaged in the brain and no one knew what it was at the hospital, only the name, Schizencephaly.

He calmed me down in his gentle way, and out of the grief I had in my heart came uncontrollable laughter when he said, "It's ok Tricia, we only use part of our brain anyway." And with that simple statement I realized I needed to get myself together and fight for this child.

I returned to my OB the following Monday. He was already standing in the room with the hospital report. His words, as I stood in the doorway, shook me to my core. "If this was my wife, I would tell her to abort." Without even acknowledging the statement, I picked up my records and walked out the door. He had already decided this pregnancy was doomed, and now I had no idea what to do except walk away and wait until it was time to deliver.

Years later I walked into that doctor's office and asked if he remembered Noah. With a room full of patients he said, "Of course, how is he?" I replied, "Do you remember telling me to abort him?" I was pleased to see the look on his face as the room emptied. It was the same look I had when he told me to abort Noah.

The violence at home became much more intense. My husband (now ex) was constantly belittling me, physically assaulting me, and the most degrading of all, spitting on me every time I walked into the room. I am not sure why he was unable to help me gather info and try to research Schizencephaly with me. I suppose he was just angry, angrier than ever before. I felt alone and starting to reconsider my doctor's words. Should I abort? I was already living in hell because of our destructive relationship, and being deprived from my friends and family in many ways.

After three days of agonizing abuse, and little support from my family, I finally had to do something I never thought I would and make the decision to end Noah's life. It seemed this was what everyone thought was right, including my own doctor. I was fighting this battle alone, and I was told Noah would never live one minute. I drove up to the abortion clinic shaking and barely able to stand. I felt like I was an animal and this was my hell. I stood there watching the people laughing as they were walking inside, like this was normal. They would be free in a few hours. I could not understand the way that felt. I couldn't even prepare myself for the moments after this would happen.

Then I felt a hand on my shoulder, and a man whispered, "Your child needs you to be strong. Do not quit on him." I never saw his face as he walked away, but I pulled my bags up and walked around the block a few times. I heard all the voices of those telling me I was not good enough to care for this child, and I became angry. By the third lap around, I had already begun to make a plan of just how I was going to do this. I found a new doctor named Dr. Jack. He was warm and understanding. I had finally found someone that was telling me I was going to be alright, and no one could tell me this child had a death sentence.

The next few months went by with me spending hours researching and blocking out all the negative people in my life, including my husband.

On May 19, 2000, I started having contractions and drove to the hospital, preparing myself for the worst. My doctor kept smiling at me saying, "I cannot wait to meet Noah." That was the only thing keeping me sane, aside from my mom and dad sitting close by.

I was told by two neurosurgeons that Noah would immediately be taken for surgery because they had determined he had Bilateral Schizencephaly, and would more than likely need a shunt for water on the brain. It was the most frightening, yet exciting, day of my life. For once I let all the control go and just prayed like never before. I prayed, "God, please let this child be guided by you. And if he is not to live more than a minute, at least let me hold him and let him know he is so very loved."

Noah came into this world very excited and vocal at 1:13 A.M. There were over eight people in the room to help. When he was whisked away to be weighed and scored, the doctor turned to me with tears in his eyes and said, "He is beautiful." It was that very moment Noah was placed in my arms, and I met the most beautiful soul I have ever seen. He was perfection.

Within minutes he was taken off to surgery, and I wouldn't let fear take over. I knew he had already beaten the odds. It was 2:30 A.M., and my baby had all his toes and fingers, and scored 9.9 on his Apgar. He was alive well for over one hour!

Noah's neurologists returned with Noah two hours later. I was told he beat another obstacle by not requiring surgery and being able to go home. It was as though everything was going to be alright. I had to stop thinking about whatever was going on in his head, and start immediately planning therapies and help to give him the best life possible.

I did think the abuse would end after Noah's birth, but it continuously got worse. Noah was constantly crying for hours on end. Between the crying and the constant physical abuse, I really began feeling like I was headed towards a meltdown. It got so bad I had to cancel Noah's therapy appointments because of black eyes and embarrassment.

When Noah was four months old, it seemed like he never stopped crying. At times I found myself screaming at the top of my lungs or throwing eggs in the woods just to get some sanity. I had no idea what was going on; he looked healthy, and doctors were baffled, but it went on day and night. My husband was no help. He would leave the house, stranding me and the boys by ourselves, for hours to days at a time. Often I would just sit, staring at Noah in tears, not knowing how to "fix" him. It truly took every bit of energy out of me. I had to either swing him or have him in my arms, and even then he was fussy. By the fourth month it was so stressful, I had to seriously contemplate if I was going to make it.

I now realize looking back, and being older, the need for stimulation from the swing and to be close by my side was due to Noah's poor vision. Even though I was told Noah was blind, I would play with light and he would respond. I knew they were wrong, but try telling that to a doctor. It was then I knew I was going to have to be the one to learn about Schizencephaly, since no doctor seemed to have a clue what to expect. They were all going by textbooks and what little information was available. I was actually seeing just how wrong both reference books and the medical field were.

I didn't talk to friends. The ex-husband would leave me with no phone, no car, no way to walk away from the intense noise in my head, and self-doubt started to return. I broke down late one night when everyone was sleeping and set up a meeting with a Christian adoption agency that did open adoption. I kept thinking I was alone and not capable of this anymore. I worried for Noah, and I worried I was stuck in a situation I was unsuited for. What happened next would shape our lives forever.

My husband was eager to sign over Noah, and I was a mess as I huddled in my bed the day he was taken. I thought it felt right; but my heart just was so overpowered with grief. Even though everyone knew I had made this choice, no one in the family came to tell Noah goodbye. It was as though everyone had left me and given up on him since birth. Now I was losing my soul. I signed the papers as my husband smiled and said it was the right thing to do. Then I lay in bed and shook for hours. Noah had left my home, but was still very much in my heart.

The state of Florida has very strict rules on contacting foster care parents, so even one hour after he was gone I wanted and tried desperately to find him. I cannot express that feeling to anyone. It was sheer panic. I managed to calm myself and placed River, my oldest son, in the car to get out of the house for a few minutes. When I put him in the car he looked up at me with his sweet voice and asked, "Where is my Brother?" I lost it and began having a full-on panic attack in the middle of the street. How on Earth did I let this happen?!

That night I was on the phone, pleading for my son back and begging them to understand how badly I needed him. Noah and River were the only things I had to define me. After three days of constant pleading phone calls, they agreed that after I got a good plan started for stress and management of Noah, they would return him.

It took two months to get Noah home. I would lay awake, day and night, thinking how happy I would be to smell and touch Noah again. River and I would sing songs about him. And although looking at pictures was hard, we had to just to remind ourselves how we would be a family again. It was the longest two months of my life!

The day they pulled up, Noah was bundled in blankets because it was cold that day. I ran out the door with bare feet, and as I did, the foster mother turned Noah to me. That was the day Noah gave us his first smile. This was the beginning of something really huge for us. That was the day I vowed that no matter what, I was never leaving this child's side again.

Years later I found out that the foster mom whom had changed our lives forever was also so touched by my determination and Noah's sweet soul, she adopted her own Schiz baby two years after she met us. They live two towns away.

I ended up leaving my husband in 2003, and I never looked back. And since that day, he has never wanted anything to do with the kids. In late 2003, Noah was still not walking and definitely not talking, but he was doing fairly well and was a very happy baby. It was heartbreaking to see him struggle to move, and it was very apparent by age three he would not ever walk on his own. His right side was almost completely paralyzed, and his eyes were constantly shifting. We had to patch them and try to control the lazy eye. I would tuck his MRI pictures away because when I would see that he was missing over 40% of his brain I would start panicking again. So those pictures were never looked at until Noah was much older.

His disability was also becoming more apparent to others. I was getting stares and told, "I'm sorry," so much I rarely went out. We were just barely making it while I went to real estate school, and I was doing it all on my own because I was too scared to ask for help. There were many nights spent crying, especially with the thought of Noah never being like other children.

His first surgery was Botox at age three to try and get him to use his right arm. It did help the tightness, but he still could not grasp toys or focus, and all he wanted to do was be by my side. He cried anytime I left the room, and even when I was in it. I know he wanted to communicate, but it just was so frustrating for us both.

It was that same year Noah began a new obstacle, seizures. During his first one I just stood there looking at him, thinking it looked like he was possessed. It only lasted a few minutes, but I was so frightened I called 911 and they came immediately.
We went through several days at the hospital. This continued this for years.

In 2007, I decided to do something for Noah. I was still angry at all the people who said he would never live, and the seizures and surgeries for muscles began making me so determined to find some answers. I knew I could not sit back and watch him die! I was set on proving everyone wrong and finding out how to fix him. I knew no other parents, and tried to read and study as much as I could. Then one day at trip to the local store, I realized I could not shop with Noah's wheelchair. I began inventing an easier way for parents to go to the store. I was creating all this in hopes I could get enough money to start research and help Noah, since medical field still had no more information than they did in 2000.

The entire year of 2008 was filled with tests, over 100 seizures at a time, constant worry, no sleep, and on top of it all, trying to maintain a job and get funds for Noah to get good medical care. Doctors in the hospitals kept telling me they could do nothing. The clefts in his brain made his seizures impossible to control. It was so bad, I forgot to eat and drink and I could never sleep for fear Noah would die in his sleep from seizing.

The day of December 7, 2008, was the worst of them all. Noah was on my bed and I turned away to do some laundry, by the time I glanced back, he was foaming and blue. He was given emergency meds to break the seizure, but nothing happened. I had a dead phone (of all days), and ran screaming down the road to call 911.

The paramedics arrived within a few minutes. By then, Noah's limp body was blue and blotchy, and he was twitching with foam coming out of his mouth. His nose was bleeding and his breathing was shallow. I followed the ambulance, watching them work on him in front of me.

When I ran into the room, every paramedic had dropped to their knees. Noah had died. I was not there and he was gone. His body was still for seconds. I fell into my father's arms, and screamed so loud, my family in the parking lot heard me. I kept screaming, "Do something!!" They just said they couldn't. We all prayed and in that very minute, Noah took a deep breath, like the wind had been knocked out of him. My father had been holding me and was white, not realizing Noah was back and breathing. It was too much for dad, and he, being the kind soul and very sensitive person he was, kept saying he could not handle this. Finally, Noah was turning back to his normal color. He let out a big laugh as I walked over to him. It was by far the scariest and most amazing thing I have ever experienced in my life.

I was able to take Noah home that night, and along the way I got a phone call from a referred doctor from the hospital, Preshant Desai, who informed me he would be happy to see Noah, and he WOULD get his seizures controlled. It was the first doctor that had given me hope and explained that seizures can be controlled. And now I felt as though everything was going to be ok. This doctor told me we would try several different medications, and Noah would not have to live like this. I was able to sleep for once, and did because with Noah's high doses of Valium, I knew he would be ok through the night. That was the first calm night I had had in four years. Little did I know it was about to change

At 12 A.M. I received a call. My dad had not returned home that night. I threw the kids back in the car, as exhausted as we were. I was driving frantically from my house to the areas he lived in, looking in ditches. I was looking in parking lots thinking maybe he had a heart attack or had been robbed. Then I remembered our special place. I drove to the woods close by dad's house where he and I would drink coffee and laugh and talk about things only we related too. He was one of the most important people in my life. So many days and nights we would sit there in those woods, talking about anything and everything.

I pulled up to what looked like a horror film with police lights flashing, and people and police tape scattered all over the place. I ran up screaming "That is my daddy's truck!" I was greeted by an officer that informed me my father had killed himself. Along with that, a note was placed in my hand. It read, "I just cannot take any more pain for Noah. "

In some ways I think a big part of my heart died that day, but I still had to keep going because Noah needed me. I imagine this would devastate most people, and in many ways it did. But after a few days of shock wearing off, I then realized if the pain was too much for him, I must be a wall of brick. In time the pain left, and I was faced with the facts that I only had my boys and mom now.

After meeting with Noah's new neurologist, his seizures were controlled, life became sane, and I began fighting hard for Noah's voice. Along the way I found other parents. And in my research, was able to see there were many other faces to Schizencephaly. Some worse, some better, but all family. It pushed me even further into doing something for the children and young adults living with this. In time we began making our company a part of all of their lives by making it a nonprofit for research. It was through the several surgeries and endless seizing that I thought I was so alone, but I had found that there were many of us seeking help. So my dream of helping Noah became a passion and a need to help others, and that is why I believe Noah was placed here. God knew I would never stop fighting, and knew I would find others to fight for. The future that six year old told my parents about had become a reality and a desire to help all children like Noah.

Noah is now 12. He should have never been here. I have fought since the day I found out his diagnosis and told he would die upon birth. He is a miracle. Even now, as strong as I am, I lay awake in constant fear of wondering how long he will be here. How long will I get to see his beautiful smile, hold his tiny hands, and kiss him every night? The fear parents live when they have a child with these issues is overwhelming. I no longer wonder if he will walk. He is still not able to talk, but we know what we are saying to each other, and he understands every word. He reaches for my hand and he guides me. This love is something no one knows except the mom of a special needs child. And I know he will not be here forever. I am not afraid to say I know one day seizures or effects from meds will take him away, but for now I just continue to fight for him and the other children that need a voice. For the ones that have passed away, we keep pictures to remind us that they are guiding us into finding cures, awareness, and hope.

Noah had surgery last month on his right leg because his scoliosis is getting to the point that everything is shifting. I hate that part about this disorder. After surgery, Noah refused all drinking. After 12 years of pride and hope that I could keep him off a feeding tube, one had to be placed for him. He seems to be heading back to his old self again, but any decision like that always places more worry into your heart as a parent. I will always choose quality and quantity for him. It's my duty as his only caregiver to make sure that his decisions are always acknowledged in life as well.

The seizures took a huge toll on Noah's body and he was never quite the same. He never got the communication I hoped for, and they certainly took many of his gross motor skills away; but today Noah can communicate through an iPad and is always smiling. I have never met such a happy little soul.

I am a proud mom who has always known this journey would be mine. And I count my blessings every day that Noah is able to give me that first smile of the morning. God, I am lucky to know someone this pure, this loving. I am the lucky one to know such an smile through his pain. I have learned to not ask why anymore, and accept the fact this path was known to me from a very young age. I just never realized how beautiful the climb would be. When I see Noah go through surgeries for his back and legs, and have to take over 11 pills a day, I sometimes wonder why his small body has to go through all this.

I realize how amazing and strong he is, and how he is here to leave a mark in this world, if not just a tiny footprint. Noah was never a mistake as I was told, but a child born with a purpose. Loaned to me from above to change this world somehow, and he is. With a body unable to move and a voice that is still unheard, his message is living proof we all have a deep meaning in this world. This journey has been one of deep spiritual growth and many disappointments. None of which ever overshadowed our achievements.

Someone once said Noah would never live past his first decade. I still like to think Noah has a mind of his own. A beautiful mind with a big mission he has only just begun. He has proven so many wrong, and doctors are often surprised by his abilities, not his inabilities. There has to be answers. So many of us are learning from our own experiences. Too many people misdiagnosed and being told bad information because Schizencephaly is so rare no one thinks there should be research. We are often the ones to correct doctors and tell them how things really are. We spent three years convincing the eye doctor Noah was not angel that can blind. He kept insisting we were wrong until he walked into Noah's patient room one day and saw the T.V. remote where the sound comes from on Noah's bed, and Noah looking up laughing at the T.V. that was over 20 feet away. That was the first apology I ever got from a doctor. Like I said, these kids prove everyone wrong, and there is not one text book that has accurately explained Noah to me yet.

Every night Noah takes my hand and holds it. It has become his way of saying goodnight. Amazing, the way he communicates with me through his eyes and movements. We have learned our own language and there are no more crying fits. We understand one another now. Although there is always fear, it is nothing like the first few years of his life. I know now that nothing could have kept us apart. He and I were supposed to know each other because we both have a journey in life. We have been so lucky to have met many families now, and Noah receives cards and loving messages from all over the world. I am often amazed how so many people have been brought together by him. I do not think I have any power in it all, I truly think I am just his vehicle and he tells me where to go.

Once upon a time I thought life was all about taking the easy road, until I met Noah, my angel with a broken wing.

Dr. Desai has been so moved by Noah's journey that he wanted to add to Noah's story.

Noah was born with a brain anomaly (birth defect) that is known as Schizencephaly, in his case bilateral open lip Schizencephaly, with diminutive optic nerves. It was actually diagnosed before birth by prenatal ultrasound at 5 months of gestation. So when he came into this world, his mother was prepared beforehand with the knowledge of his condition, and clued into its potential implications. While nobody without direct or indirect experience of raising such a special child can be fully aware or prepared for its challenges, his mother gladly give him her all, and he reciprocated likewise.

By age 3 yrs old he was noted to be able to take assisted steps using a walker, but his spasticity prevented him from progressing further. He remained non-verbal, and his visual tracking has been inconsistent. He has required total-care.

His seizures began around age 7 years, with grand mal convulsions, and brief myoclonic spasms. There were multiple visits to the emergency room. At the time he was first evaluated in my office, his seizure medication was switched from Trileptal to Lamictal, and Keppra was added soon thereafter. He actually became seizure-free within a few months, but as is frequently the case with Schizencephaly his seizures relapsed. His medications were maximized, and eventually required addition of Phenobarb and Clonazepam, before seizure control was re-established. Occasional attempts to wean him down on his seizure meds have resulted in seizure recurrence, and as long as he is maintained on his current combination, he does very well. There has not been any ER visit in a long time.

Currently 12 years old, Noah is a delightful child, with an infectious smile that lights up the room (and his mother's heart) and spreads joy to all around him. He has no expectations.

His heart is pure.

He may not have the tools that we take for granted, he may not stand or walk or talk, and he may not converse, but he has a special mission. He was born for a higher purpose: to hold up a mirror to ourselves, to enable us to be better and nobler, to spread the awareness that just like him, we are here transiently for a reason: to rise beyond ourselves and realize our true potential. Will we?

Prashant Desai, M.D.
Pediatric Neurology

TRICIA DENNIS and STEPHANIE ZIEMANN

Ada-Lily

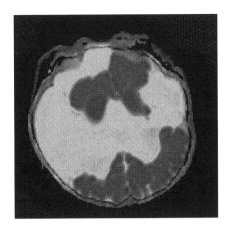

Ada-Lily was very much a planned baby. My husband and I talked about having kids very early on in our relationship. When we decided it was time to start trying, I had my birth control removed, was eating healthy, and started taking prenatal vitamins. I tested positive four months later on October 30, 2009, and we were ecstatic.

My pregnancy wasn't the easiest, but it wasn't the worst. One of the things I had to deal with was an extreme case of morning sickness. I couldn't eat, smell, talk, stand up, take a shower, or walk without having to be ill. This lasted four months, until I finally got medication to stop the sickness because I had started throwing up blood. And there was also a miscarriage scare.

The first OBGYN appointment I had wasn't until early December, but a few days before that I had gone to the emergency room because I was bleeding. They told me that I was probably having a miscarriage; there was nothing they could do for me, and to follow up with my OB. When I went to my doctor they did an ultrasound, he said everything was fine. I had some blood work done that showed I was RH- and that's what was causing the bleeding. The doctor said that if the hospital had done blood work like they should have, they would have seen that I was RH- and could have given me a shot that night. Other than that, I had the normal aches and pains of pregnancy.

My due date was July 6, 2010, but because the back and hip pain I was having caused me to barely be able to walk, my doctor decided to induce me early. It was only two days early, but two days less that I had to be pregnant. I was started on Pitocin at 10:30 in the morning on the 4th of July, and after a very short labor, Ada-Lily was born that night at 8:50 P.M.

From the very start she was screaming. I dismissed it, thinking that the new experiences of the outside world (the pressure of gravity, sights, smells, sounds, lights, hot, cold, hunger, and textures of the fabric of her clothing) were overbearing for a newborn. But it never ended. It got so bad that on her second day, the nurses begged me to let them take her so that I could get some sleep. I had clearly stated beforehand in my birth plan (that everyone had a copy of) that after Ada was born, she was to NOT leave my room without me or her father; but I had not slept since she was born, so I agreed to let them take her for the night. The night didn't last long. The nurses brought Ada back in less than two hours because she was screaming and they couldn't calm her down.

Ada screamed so much and so hard, that she had burst blood vessels in her eyes. Never once did they check her out or think there could be something wrong with her. They did however question me and accuse me of doing drugs during my pregnancy because her screaming was a common sign of babies whom were going through withdrawals, and took some more blood for testing. The nurses took blood before they induced me and the morning after I gave birth for testing. I guess they thought I had somehow smuggled drugs into the hospital. Of course the tests came back clear. I've never even smoked a cigarette; I definitely wasn't doing drugs during my pregnancy.

When we went home, things got worse. Ada-Lily would always scream. Not cry. Scream. And not only a few hours a day, more like 18 hours a day. If she was up and wasn't eating, she was screaming. For the first two weeks I kept telling myself what I told myself at the hospital, the new experiences of the outside world were overwhelming; but after those two weeks were up, I had to stop lying to myself. I knew there was something wrong with my baby. I would call her doctor and tell him what was going on. He'd say it was colic or thrush and send us home.

Then we got another doctor. This one said it was colic, gas, the need to poop, we were being over-reactive first-time parents, and finally, that we were just bad parents. Then he too would send us home. Even after I had voiced my concerns about Ada being three months old and not being able to hold her head up, unclench her fists, and that she was becoming severely cockeyed, the doctor never listened to me. He never offered to do any testing, or gave us any explanations.

We also tried the ER. They would say she needs to poop, like the rest. Or they would scratch their heads and shrug their shoulders at us. One doctor told me that all of our problems would be solved if I learned how to properly swaddle a baby. We paid $80 for that prestigious piece of medical advice.

I had many OBGYN visits for the first two months after giving birth. I kept telling my doctor that there was something wrong with my baby and I needed help getting someone who will listen to me. All he did was tell me I couldn't handle being a first-time mother, I had severe Postpartum Depression, and kept giving me higher and higher doses of Prozac every visit. I felt ignored and like my concerns were attempted to be snuffed out with medication.

We were also having problems with eating. I tried so hard for six weeks to breastfeed. We saw a couple of lactation specialists and I was on two different medications that were supposed to increase my milk supply. Ada would never latch on correctly, no matter what I did. She would "chomp" instead of suck, and my milk never really came in.

Her pediatrician, my OB, and the lactation specialist all kept urging me to continue to breastfeed. Ada had gone from her birth weight of 7 pounds 5 ounces, to barely 7 pounds, and she looked so frail. Ada-Lily was a month and a half old, and still wearing preemie clothing. To continue to breastfeed would mean starving my baby to death, and all the professionals wanted me to continue to starve her. They were saying that even though I was on two medications for milk supply, feeding her every other hour for an hour, and pumping almost the entire hour she wasn't feeding, that I wasn't doing enough. Not only was it slowly killing Ada, but it was taking a toll on me. Finally my husband said enough, no more breastfeeding, and we switched to formula. She still never latched onto the bottle or learned to suck instead of "chomp." That never seemed to raise any concern in the pediatrician either.

The screaming was nonstop. The blood vessels in Ada's eyes kept bursting. She was throwing up from all the screaming and would sometimes pass out. One night, I couldn't take it anymore. I called my mother in tears and said that I was going to leave and never come back. She called my husband, Jeremy, and told him to get home ASAP. He tried to calm Ada down for hours to no avail. I wanted to take her to the hospital as soon as he came home, but we had just gone to the pediatrician and the hospital a couple of days before, only to be sent home with no answer other than, "She needs to poop." Jeremy didn't want to waste another five hours and $80 to be told the same thing again.

It had been three and a half months and she kept screaming. One night in October of 2010, Ada was doing her usual ear-piercing, blood curdling, horrifying screams until she couldn't breathe. Her eyes rolled in the back of her head and she went limp. We thought she was dead. We got her to wake up and we were greeted with more screams. We packed up and went to the hospital, again. On the way to the hospital, I called the after-hours number for her pediatrician. When I finally got ahold of the doctor, he acted as though he had no idea who we were. He said that he has never seen our daughter, and if he has, we have never mentioned her screaming to him. He ended by saying we were overreacting, but if we really felt the need to go to a hospital then that's what we should do, and hung up on me.

The hospital was going to send us home (with the poop excuse again) when another doctor ordered an X-ray of Ada's stomach. While we were waiting for the results of the X-ray, a nurse came in to talk to me because they could tell that I needed help. They asked me if I was suicidal and I told them that I didn't want to be here anymore. I didn't have any specific plans, but I would like very much to go to sleep and never wake up. They asked if I would be willing to check myself in, with a cop standing outside the room. At that point I knew it was stay voluntarily or against my will. I agreed.

The results of Ada's X-ray back, they thought she had something wrong with her intestines and said she needed to go to a separate hospital because they couldn't take care of her at the one we were at. The doctor assured me that it was easily fixable, and if it was severe enough that it needed surgery, it was a simple procedure. I didn't fight being checked in myself and staying in a separate hospital because of that doctors words. I regret still that.

The next day, a caseworker came in to tell me that: 1) Child Protective Services (CPS) was called because a case worker that was at the other hospital with my husband and daughter had called them and told them that I had said I wanted to kill my daughter. And 2) My daughter has 40% of her brain and has only two years to live.

I was absolutely livid for so many reasons. I was yelling at my caseworker to get the woman who had NEVER talked to me over here so that I can set her straight and find out where she gets off on calling CPS and quoting me on something that I had never said, and never would say, when she had never seen me or even talked to me.

Then the second half of what she said dawned on me. I felt the ice-cold shock of fear. Question after question flew out of my mouth, and this poor woman who had just received my wrath moments before was now in tears because she had no answers for me. She gave me two printouts on Ada's condition and said that she needed to leave.

Those printouts were all the information I had about what was going on with my baby. No one had answers, and my husband didn't even know there was a diagnosis yet. I was somehow the first person to be given the diagnosis, and I was in a separate hospital on the other end of town. I read the diagnosis, Schizencephaly, and the few short paragraphs of lacking information over the phone to Jeremy. We were both lost and frightened. Those feelings were amplified by our inability to be there for one another.

After a couple more days of me being hospitalized, my doctor from the hospital concluded that I had Postpartum Depression, and with everything that was going on, I had had a nervous breakdown. My doctor decided that I needed to be with my family more than I needed to be kept prisoner because she knew that most of the issues I was having were rooted in not getting the help I was so desperately seeking. She gave me yet another prescription for a higher dosage of Prozac, and I was released to be with my daughter and husband.

While all that was going on with me, Jeremy had a lot going on as well. The first night at the new hospital Ada was relocated to; they did some tests and more X-rays, and were going to send him home because they didn't see anything wrong. Then our savior, Ada-Lily's current pediatrician, came in to do his rounds. According to my husband, when the pediatrician came into the room he woke up Ada, took one look at her eyes, and ordered a CT scan. The CT scan showed that she only had 40% of her brain (which they say is a generous estimate). They did two MRI's to make sure that what they were seeing on the CT scan wasn't a mistake, and two EEG's (one with 24 hour video) to check for seizure activity.

The results were that Ada had Schizencephaly. Bilateral Open-Lip Schizencephaly. The neurologist said that because of the little amount of brain that Ada had, she should be blind, deaf, unable to move, she won't be able to talk, never walk, never feed herself, won't have a personality, will never eat solid foods, tell the difference between pain and pleasure (if she could feel anything at all), and countless other things that we take for granted every day. All of the doctors agreed that the fact that Ada could follow a person walking across the room with her eyes, turn her head to look for a familiar voice, and something as simple as smile and breathe on her own, were against the odds. We were told that Ada-Lily had two years to live, if that. And the best that we can hope for was that she would stop breathing (because that is how she would go, according to the neurologist) in her sleep and not suffer. I felt like I was having my fortune told by the world's worst fortune teller. It's like knowing how and when you will die, only far worse. We decided to try and put that out of our minds as much as we could. We were going to enjoy life and fill Ada-Lily with love until she burst with it.

The neurologist called me out into the hallway to show me Ada's MRI. The images went one at a time, from front to back. Ada's entire frontal lobe is absent, and it felt like forever before we caught a glimpse of brain matter instead of fluid. My knees buckled, my legs turned to jello, I couldn't breathe, and my entire body felt like I had jumped into a pool of ice water. All I could think was, "This can't be real. There is no way anyone could live with that little of their brain." That was one of the worst moments of my life.

The night I was told about Ada's prognosis, I called my boss and told her everything we had found out. She knew right away that I was leaving my job. I thought she was going to be angry, but she knew that my place was at home with my baby, spending every precious minute I had with Ada. Not many bosses, even ones that are parents themselves, fully understand the need for a parent to be home to take care of their child. That need to be home is far greater when the child needs round-the-clock care.

While we were at the hospital Ada was in, we spoke with numerous doctors, caseworkers, people that ran support programs, and countless others. We talked to a female medical caseworker who didn't understand how we had no idea that our daughter was going to be born this way because it was something that is easily visible on an ultrasound. She became even more puzzled when I told her that I had an ultrasound at every single visit to the OB, and nothing was ever mentioned. The caseworker looked into it and talked to my OB. She found out that, yes, he did know about this, but he chose not to share that information with us because he felt that we would have had an abortion and he does not agree with abortions.

I was enraged. I felt that what he did was wrong and cruel. The choice to continue the pregnancy was mine and my husband's, not his. The fact that he took that choice upon himself and decided that we were to give birth to a disabled baby. To break our hearts every single moment of every single day, and cause Ada to suffer her entire life, is a decision that he should have to pay for. Unfortunately, the courts don't see it that way. We are very lucky that Ada is doing as well as she is, but things could have turned out much worse, and we were never given the chance to decide for ourselves what to do or to prepare ourselves for the future as much as possible. I sat in front of my OB numerous times crying about how my daughter was always screaming, never happy, and that I knew something was wrong with my baby, but no one would listen to me. Not even then did he try to hint that I was right, that my baby had a severe brain malformation and he knew about it, and that we should go to the hospital to have them look at her brain. Never once did he try to help us. The OB could have tossed me a bone, saying that it sounds like something neurological and to go get a CT scan. Something, *anything*, to help us would have been gracious, but he wasn't. At the very least, he should have been reprimanded for the unethical actions he took, but there was nothing I could do.

Only one day after I got out of the hospital, Ada was released. We were sent home with a new pediatrician, a neurologist, a neurosurgeon, an ophthalmologist, a caseworker, and an appointment for Help Me Grow. My head was swimming with information, names, numbers, appointment dates, diagnoses, questions, and on top of it all, fear and grief. The day we came home, the old pediatrician (the one that had no clue who we were, and had claimed to have never seen my daughter) had the nerve to call because he was informed of Ada's hospital stay and the hospital's findings. He wanted to make sure we were going to do a follow up with him. My husband told him what we thought about him, and in case that wasn't enough, he also made it very clear that we would never set foot in that doctor's office again. It was better that Jeremy talked to that doctor and not me. Jeremy was far more cordial than I would have been.

We were home from the hospital in time for Ada's first Halloween. My parents had driven up from North Carolina to be with us that weekend. They were hoping to make it up while Ada was still in the hospital to help Jeremy out, but their jobs didn't consider Ada's ordeal to be an emergency. Jeremy and I were exhausted from all the stress we were under, and my parents were exhausted from their long trip. We bought Ada a cute Halloween outfit and pajama set, stayed home, and loved on the princess. That was a satisfactory enough Halloween celebration for all of us.

Even though we now knew Ada had Schizencephaly and her screaming was most likely a neurological misfire, we still had nothing to help her. It wasn't until she was six months old that her neurologist gave us Klonopin, a muscle relaxer/seizure preventative/antidepressant, that would also help with the screaming. And it did. I was happy and at the same time upset because they had not given this miracle medicine to us sooner.

Things were fine for a while, not great, but fine. The screaming had ceased. Now when Ada cried, she cried for a reason. Crying was something we could handle with no problem, and were thankful for. Ada started to have in-home physical and speech therapy once a week, and Help Me Grow came out every two weeks. She still could not hold her head up or unclench her fists, and she still didn't eat from the bottle correctly.

We applied for SSI for Ada-Lily shortly after coming home from the hospital in November 2010, and we were told that she had been accepted. I went to the social security office downtown to fill out some forms. While I was there, I was informed that she would be receiving $674 a month. I was told how it was to be spent, how to keep track of the expenditures, and how to open an account just for Ada when I got the first check. The worker said that we would be getting Ada's first check the week of Christmas.

Christmas came and went with no arrival of a check. It wasn't until the week of New Year's that we received anything. We finally got what we thought was going to be her check, but instead was a letter of rejection. The letter stated that Ada was "accepted" because of her disability, but denied funds because my husband makes too much money. They knew how much money he was making when the man told me that we were accepted, and now it's too much? I called the number on the letter and the woman that I talked to said that we made too much, and that if for whatever reason my husband lost his job or got laid off we could try to reapply. Until then we're out of luck until she turns 18.

I went down one last time for SSI. This time I talked to a woman worker. She was nice enough to tell me to give up. Unless my husband lost his job, (and if he did, he would have to be unemployed for six months before we could apply for SSI again), or died, or Ada turned 18, we had no chance for help. And that if I was so bad off, I should go apply for food stamps. Or, better yet, get a job and work for what I want, like everyone else in this world has to do.

Once again, I went straight for a lawyer. There are only two lawyers in Toledo that could handle Ada's case. You can't call just any lawyer that deals with Social Security cases when it involves a child, you have to have a lawyer that deals specifically with juvenile Social Security cases, and there were only two of them. They also said the same thing, that Social Security was like Welfare, it was meant only for those in poverty, and we could try again when she turns 18. No one seems to care that the basic necessities these children need is enough to put you in poverty.

We decided to throw Ada-Lily a half birthday party. I know, it sounds ridiculous. I had been joking about having one for her since I read that it was "all the rage" in a parenting magazine while I was pregnant. However, after all that we had been through, and the grim prognosis that was given to Ada, the half birthday party seemed like something that we should do, and something that would lift our spirits. I baked a cake, frosted it, cut it in half, and wrote "Happy Half Birthday Ada-Lily!" on it. It wasn't a big celebration, just Ada-Lily,

Jeremy, my brother, my brother's two children, and myself. It was nice, and it did make us feel slightly better for the moment.

From then on, nothing out of the normal happened until March 2011. Ada-Lily hadn't been feeling very well and would not take the bottle at all. Every time we put the bottle in her mouth, she would cry. She didn't have a fever, and I knew that as long as this only lasted a day or two and she was still wetting diapers, she would be ok. Around six in the evening, Ada had a diaper with a dark yellow, almost orange, residue that smelled foul. My mother (who was in town visiting to help us move) and I took Ada to the hospital. They put her on an IV, put fluids in her, and sent us home. We spent the entire month of April in and out of the hospital because Ada would not take the bottle. I had a special bottle that I could squirt the formula into Ada's mouth, but even then she choke on it and wouldn't drink. I was spending up to four hours trying to feed Ada two ounces of food. In the end, my husband and I decided to have a feeding tube placed.

On April 30, 2011, Ada went in for surgery to have the feeding tube placed. The surgery time was shorter than expected and we went to her room for recovery. I was instructed to try to feed Ada orally so the surgery site wouldn't be irritated. Every time we tried to feed her, she would instantly vomit up everything she had taken in. She was also back to screaming like she used to scream. I kept telling all the doctors and nurses that there was something wrong and I wanted Ada's tube to be inspected. They assured me that it was a simple procedure and there could be nothing wrong. After three days of this, they decided to "amuse" me (as they said) and take Ada down to get X-rays. As it turns out, they had indeed botched up a "simple procedure." A procedure that was so simple that we should have been home the day after surgery. The balloon was in her intestine when they inflated it, keeping the tube lodged in there. Never once did we receive an apology for their mistake that was causing my child extreme pain. We went home a few days later, angry and without any acknowledgment of their wrongdoing.

We still struggle with doctors that don't take proper care of Ada. We've walked out on four ophthalmologist appointments (same doctor) because we sat in the waiting room for over an hour each time. Meanwhile, other patients that were there to see the same doctor were taken back no more than 10 minutes upon their arrival. The last time we walked out I had left messages for the ophthalmologist to call me back. She returned my call one week later with excuses that it wasn't her fault, she can't control the people that work for her, and she strongly advised that we stay with her. I asked her how the work ethic of her employees was of no fault of her own. Did she not keep a daily copy of her own schedule? Did she not notice when scheduled patients failed to be in her office? And I told her that if she had put any effort into making sure that things were running properly, or came out to see if we were running late to the appointment, she would have seen us sitting impatiently in the waiting room with a crying baby.

Not only did we receive bad service with that ophthalmologist, but she also could have been making Ada's vision worse. Ada is legally blind, but she isn't living in darkness. The first ophthalmologist said that Ada was farsighted and needed glasses, and we needed to patch her eyes. The new ophthalmologist gave us completely different information. Ada was farsighted, but she was well within the range of sight that she didn't need glasses or patching. Wearing glasses when she didn't need them would only further damage her eyes, and the patching would never do her any good because she is unable to focus on objects long enough to make it effective. We had been wasting a lot of time and money.

The latest big disturbance that has happened to us is Ada started having seizures. Because of the severity of the malformations of her brain, she should have been seizing from birth, but she staved them off for almost two years. Late June 2012, Ada had her first seizure, and it was terrifying. Her back arched, her arms and legs went straight out and stiffened, and her eyes were distant and unseeing. When she came to, she made a scream that I've never heard her make before, and then vomited. I had seen someone seize before because my mother has seizures, but this was my baby, and no matter how prepared I thought I was, I wasn't. We got the soonest available appointment for the neurologist and started messing around with medications. There's a combination that seems to be working well. She was having upwards of 20 seizures a day, but now there haven't been any seizures for a while. The seizures also added two more diagnoses to Ada-Lily's list of disabilities; Cerebral Palsy and Epilepsy.

Unfortunately, we can't get any help in the sleeping

department. Sleeplessness seems to be a common symptom of Schizencephaly. Ada will go to bed around 10 P.M. She usually wakes up anywhere between 2 - 4 A.M., and goes back to sleep two to three hours after waking up, but will only sleep for another couple of hours. They don't make sleeping medications for children, and adult sleeping medications inhibit the brain from sending out growth hormones while the child sleeps. Because children grow in their sleep, the medication could cause Ada to have stunted growth, and the doctors don't want to give her anything. We might get to revisit the option of sleeping medication when Ada is seven. Until then, we give her a concoction of Melatonin, children's allergy medication, Valproic Acid, Klonopin, and Onfi to try to get and keep Ada asleep. If we can get five straight hours of sleep, it's a relief.

As Ada's second birthday crept up on us, so did the fear of losing her. We were told that she wouldn't make it to see her second birthday countless times, and I was beginning to dread the day that was coming up fast. I laid awake most nights, unable to sleep for fear that she would need me and I wouldn't be able to help. I needed to hear her breathe. If I couldn't hear Ada breathing, I had to watch to see if her chest would rise and fall. If I couldn't see her chest rise and fall, I would shake her just enough to make her move on her own. I was exhausted and terrified.

Ada's second birthday came, and she was alive. We had close family and friends over for food and cake. We didn't open any gifts because there weren't any to open, we had asked for money instead. Asking for money is so much easier than trying to explain to people what to buy, and after two years of buying infant toys (most of which Ada still can't play with) we had pretty much everything in the stores bought already. Plus sending people to special needs websites to buy a $65 switch toy or a $600 iPad is kind of a ridiculous request. What I had done was ask that if people were going to get anything, give us cash in a card and I made a card box, like you see at weddings. We did a Minnie Mouse themed party and a matching card box. And just like the card boxes at weddings, we waited until the day after the party to open up the cards to see what Ada got.

There is a lot of equipment and different braces that most children and adults with Schizencephaly need. Ada currently has two different styles of hand and feet splints, a special feeder seat, a stander, a special bath seat, and a wheelchair. We had hoped that she would be sitting up by now, but she still can't even hold her head up. In the years that come we will have to by bigger sizes of the feeder and bath seats. We might even have to look into an electric bath seat, one that rises up and down to help try and save our backs as she gets bigger. We'll also have to look into a lift to pick her up for us. We have a van, but we can't afford to have it converted to be wheelchair accessible. The cheapest I've found was a quote for $15,000. That's half of what our van costs. Hopefully we can get by without needing to convert or buy an already accessible van for a few more years.

There are also many, many procedures and surgeries most children end up having. Luckily, the fluid that is in Ada's brain is perfect. There isn't too much fluid, and she doesn't have any pressure on her brain. The fluid that she has (and there is a lot of it) is filling in the empty spaces of her brain perfectly. That can change though. If, for whatever reason, she began to collect fluid in her brain, she would have to have a shunt put in to drain the fluid. Shunts are not uncommon for these children. Ada already had to have a feeding tube placed, and it is very likely that she will also need a tracheotomy done some day. The neurologist is planning on starting Botox on her legs and arms in the very near future because the muscles are so tight. Ada could take medication to relax her muscles, but she is already on so many medications as it is, and a muscle relaxer would not target only the muscles we want to relax, it would relax every muscle in her body, making her poor head and trunk support even worse. With Botox, we can target the specific muscles we need to make relax, and give the exact amount of Botox to those muscles to get the desired effect. We've tried casting (another typical procedure for these children) her legs for a week, but she's still very tight.

My husband and I go through this by ourselves for the most part, without much help from family or friends. Distant family has become even more distant, and our friends (except for the exceptional few) have become strangers. Not many people want to around you when you have a disabled child. Disabilities aren't contagious, but people act like they are. The only constant support we have is each other, Help Me Grow/Early Intervention (until Ada turns three), my mother and step-father, my grandmother, and a few close friends. Other than that, this is a very lonely life.

My parents live in North Carolina and constantly use vacation time to come up here for the important things; holidays, hospital stays, and birthdays. They work a lot of unpaid overtime because they've asked coworkers to give them (my parents) their vacation time. They also have my grandfather living with them, and to come up here means having to leave him alone, which is becoming increasingly dangerous as he ages. I have a grandmother that lives in town, but she works every chance she gets to try and save up for her retirement. My grandmother has bad legs, and she gets tired easily, so I don't want her to have to look after Ada.

Then there is my husband's family. They were at the hospital the week that we found out about Ada's condition and were told that we were going to need more support than a family with a typical child. All of them said they would be there for us and would watch Ada for us when we needed a break, but as soon as we were home from the hospital they had all but disappeared and had transparent excuses as to why they had to bail on us. Jeremy's mother would tell us, "I am taking Ada this Saturday (or some other day), and I won't take no for an answer." That Saturday (or whichever day she insisted on) would come and we would be calling her as we were on our way to the car only to have her tell us that either she had the kids from down the block or her grandson over earlier that day and she couldn't watch Ada anymore. That was if we could get ahold of her at all. There were times that we called over and over, text her, emailed her, but never heard from her. After a few months of things continuing like this (and other issues), the situation escalated to the point of no return, and we no longer have contact with his family.

After Jeremy and I said we were no longer going to deal with them, they kept saying was how hard this all was on them. Not once did they ever think about how hard this is on us. Ada is OUR child, not theirs. They don't have to watch her fail every day at holding her head up, hardly developing, unable to drink liquids or eat solid foods. They don't have to look at her and wonder if this day will be her last. They don't have to worry about where the money will come from to cover the costs of all of her medications, co-pays, and equipment. They don't have to worry about how they will afford everything Ada needs once she turns three and they no longer have Help Me Grow to help cover the costs, and there still won't be any hope for financial support from SSI. They don't have nightmares every time they close their eyes about having to bury their only child. Yet we need to consider *their* needs and allow them to continue to disrespect us? Never. Our lives are hard enough and we refuse to have anyone around that will only make it harder. I learned a long time ago that family is a privilege, not a right, and they've lost their privilege to be a part of our family. Now it's primarily the three of us, and we are just fine with that.

Ada and I tend to be in our own little world most of the time. In this world of ours, Ada-Lily is a typical child. I don't pretend that she isn't disabled, the way she is has become my normal. It isn't until we are around other people that I am brought back to reality. Seeing a younger child that already has so much more ability than Ada, or children that are around Ada's age that trigger the thoughts of,

"That's what Ada should be doing," to my mind. Sometimes it breaks my heart, and other times I put all of my focus on Ada to keep the depressing thoughts of how things should have been away. Once in a while my bubble gets a hole poked in it, the air starts to leak out and the pain seeps in.

I still have breakdowns here and there. I still cry over the things that Ada can't do, and will probably never do. I cry over the frustration of all the casts, splints, and awkwardly bulky equipment that we have to use that make Ada frustrated and uncomfortable. All the appointments I have to keep up with on a weekly basis, the medications, the what if's. I cry at the fact that I will never see my daughter walk, chase a butterfly, scrape her knee, go to her prom, fall in love, get married, or have children of her own. Then there are times I cry and I don't even know what the reason is. It's ok to cry, good even. Those feelings need to get out. When you have a disabled child you go through a mourning process. You mourn over the life that is lost to your child, the life they will never have. You also mourn the fact that you will never be a typical family, with typical family moments and memories.

It's not all heartache and strife. There are more happy days than there are sad. Like I said, we are in our own little world most of the time. We play (which is usually me having to play with toys for Ada), talk, sing, watch movies, and best of all, we laugh. Ada has a smile that lights up any bad day. Ada loves to be ticked, bounced, kissed, and snuggled. Whenever I feel down, I hold her and tell her all the reasons I love her. She usually talks back to me in her Ada-Lily way.

I am amazed by Ada every single day. I am proud of everything she does. Things that are so seemingly simple like waking up in the morning, looking and turning her head towards noises, activating a switch toy, making a sound, holding her head up for a few seconds, or swallowing without choking, are celebrated. I shower her with praise, love, and attention from the moment she opens her eyes in the morning to the moment she closes her eyes to go to sleep at night in my arms.

When I feel like I can't go on, I can't take the stress of this life, all I have to do is look at Ada, and I know I can do anything for her. Ada-Lily is my strength, my life, my reason for reason. She forces me to be strong, not only because she needs me to be, but because she is my inspiration. Ada is my hero. For so long I was lost. I was in an ocean of darkness, being pulled under by depression. Ada-Lily found me through all that darkness, and she was the shining light that brought me back to life.

I don't know how long I will have my Ada-Lily. I hope to be changing my diapers with hers, but that might not be a reality. Whether it's one year or 50 years, I want every day filled with love, affection, and smiles. I make it my main goal to do whatever it takes to make Ada happy. As long as Ada is happy, I know I'm doing all right.

TRICIA DENNIS and STEPHANIE ZIEMANN

Gage

June 17, 2008, Dustin and I welcomed Gage Rayden into the world. With an overall "normal" pregnancy, we were excited to meet our new baby boy. That was until we noticed something was wrong and no one was telling us what. Hours after my C-section they still wouldn't let us hold or even be in the same room as Gage. They kept telling us that he just wasn't thriving the way that he should and needed to rest. We went the entire night without being able to hold Gage. No one had been able to hold him except for Dustin right after he was born.

The next morning, the pediatrician came in and told us that they were going to move Gage to the nearest children's hospital. There was something wrong with our baby and they had no clue what it was. My heart sank. What could be wrong? And what was going to happen to my precious baby?

The next few days were like a whirlwind. It seemed like years before we knew what was going on, but at the same time it seemed like things were moving so fast. After the first day of being at the University of Kentucky Children's Hospital, our nurse finally came in and told us that our son would need open heart surgery, but the doctor would have to explain everything to us and he would be in as soon as he could.

Dustin and I broke down. At that moment, even though there was a room full of people, it was like we were the only two people in the whole world. There was a lot to take in when the cardiology team and surgeon came in to speak with us. Gage had a severe Aortic Coarctation and multiple holes in the bottom portion of his heart. He needed open heart surgery ASAP. The next day, at just three days old, our little boy would undergo his first of two open heart surgeries, and the first of four heart procedures.

It seems somewhat weird to me now, the sense of peace I had in my heart that night after everyone left and things began to sink in. Looking back, I believe that God had His hands on me that night, and sheltered me from my fear of what could happen to Gage while the doctors had his tiny heart stopped.

Gage's first heart surgery took over six hours, but it felt like a lifetime. When they finally called to let us know that they would be taking him to the PICU, we all ran down the stairs from the floor my hospital room was on to the hall where they would be bringing Gage down. I can remember that moment vividly; there were at least 20 people lining both sides of the hallway waiting to catch a glimpse of Gage as they brought him down. When I saw them wheeling Gage's little bed down the hallway, the tears began to roll. There he was, doctors and nurses all around, and tubes coming from everywhere. No one is ever prepared to see their child in such a state. It broke my heart looking at my small child in such bad shape.

That night we stayed by Gage's bed as long as we could, and

returned from my hospital room first thing that next morning. When we got into the PICU his nurse met us and informed us that Gage had begun to have seizures in the night. They started him on Phenobarbital, and scheduled him to have an MRI of his brain to see what was going on. Again I felt crushed; Gage had already been through so much.

Since Gage was born he has had two MRI's, and has been diagnosed with Bilateral Open-Lipped Schizencephaly, extensive stroke damage, and extensive migrational abnormalities throughout his brain. His current neurologist says that compared to his MRI, Gage is doing so much more than they would expect him to be doing. God has blessed us in so many ways with Gage.

Gage has a rather large team of doctors, and some days I find it hard to keep up with them all. We see a neurologist and a genetic doctor out of state at the Cincinnati Children's Hospital. We also see a cardiologist every few months, an ear, nose, and throat doctor (ENT), and an eye doctor that we have to see every three weeks while we prepare for Gage's eye surgery.

Gage also has a wonderful group of therapists that have been with him since he was four months old. We go to an outpatient therapy clinic twice a week and the therapists feel like family to us. They are just as excited as we are when Gage accomplishes something new, and they worry for his well-being. They have been wonderful in every way, without them I wouldn't know half the things I do. In some ways they have been more helpful than his doctors have.

I have always worried that my other two boys would resent Gage for all the attention that he has required, but it has been quite the opposite. Every day they amaze me at how much they love and care for their brother. Brett, our oldest, is like a mother hen. You can see the concern on his face at the thought of something being wrong with Gage. Even something like a cold makes Brett worry. He always tells us that he watches over Gage at school and goes by his classroom to ask teachers how he is doing. Cruz is our youngest, 14 months younger than Gage, and his shadow. He has passed Gage up developmentally in many ways, but when he sees Gage struggling, he will stop what he is doing to aid him. He does anything and everything that he can to help. It touches my heart how much love both Cruz and Brett have for their brother. I believe that the interaction and help that Brett and Cruz have given has helped him develop in a way that has surpassed both the doctor's and therapist's expectations.

We have watched our child in pain, knowing that we can't do anything to help him. We have watched him slowly develop, and be passed up in many ways by his younger brother. Gage has been through more in his little life than most people go through in an entire lifetime. His journey will be a hard one and he will have to overcome many obstacles, but he has already shown our family, and many others, that miracles DO happen. And just because the doctors say so, doesn't mean that it will be that way.

His life holds a lot of uncertainty, but we will help Gage fight to the end in any way possible because he is our shining star. He may be special needs, but he is no less than any of the rest!

Phillip

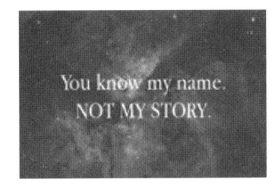

At night I often heard my mom praying in her closet to God. "God, a child is born unto this world who needs protection...please guide him and protect him."

She did not know how to accept at times that something was different and always put on a brave face. But in the night, when the memories of the day are most relevant, that is when she prayed most. I heard her on many occasions asking God for strength.

I had some learning disabilities, and of course my mom didn't want me to be in special classes. Back in the 70's and 80's, we were nowhere near acceptance like we are today. There were no support groups or awareness days. People didn't even know what ADHD was, let alone how to treat it. Basically, anyone from a stutter to a limp was placed in the same class or a special needs class. Luckily I was in mainstream classes, and I just dealt and tried to find clever ways and words to answer people's questions.

My mom pushed for me and wanted me in school like everyone else. I didn't do too well, and I seemed to learn in a different way. It's rather amazing how the brain learns to direct new paths when it is disrupted. I have to say, looking back I felt like I was wading in mud, but that made me strong and independent. And I now realize how difficult the life of a mother is. Even one without any medical issues (props to my mom).

My sister was an influence on me too. We use to fight, but ironically, she was my biggest protector in school. I got picked on and beat up a lot. Most of the teachers let it happen because back then they were not slapped with lawsuits and reprimanded for letting this stuff happen. But it made me stronger.

Once in junior high, I started to fight back with useless effort. I guess it was the will to be like everyone else. I started to try things like bicycles, skates, scooters, and just about anything else I saw other children doing. I got hurt half the time, but I was use to it and kept on trying. Throughout this whole growing process I didn't realize the symptoms of Schizencephaly because I didn't know what it was, so I didn't pay any attention to them.

In high school I realized they were not teaching me the things that interested me. One day, something just clicked in my brain as I watched my mother paint; I wanted to be an artist. I dropped out of school because I knew I had a bigger plan in life, and school is not for everyone.

Like any young adult leaving school, I was lost. I floated around, unsure of what to do. I had jobs and lost them. My dad showed me the basics about working and did what he could to get me to see how I needed to present myself. I didn't have a car, but my dad said, "You have a 10 speed to get there, so get to it." Of course he helped me get what I wanted and needed, but most of all; he showed me how to walk away from a fight but still stand up for myself. Dads are great in that way.

My biological mom was a major influence on me too. We always played paddle ball, racquetball, and our favorite, badminton. She was the athletic type and kept me aggressive. She encouraged me to always look deep inside myself, to know and be happy with who I am. These subtle things my family did without me realizing made a powerful imprint in my mind. One of the best things she told me was everything is in moderation. She gave me much insight on life, and how God leads you in the right direction if you just let him. She was the one that lead the family into the way we are now, long before I was born.

Our whole family was pretty tight. I am the youngest of five children and had a lot of encouragement from all of them. I always had my leg problems, odd things like twitches, and my body had a hard time keeping up with me. I got so use to pain that a lot was just ignored.

My mother persuaded me to go back to community college and get my diploma, which led her into actually going to college and taking graphic arts with me. Her support was amazing, and the reason I stayed interested in school. I even started helping out in class.

Things really progressed after that. I found my first real job in graphics while I was in school, and of course did what any young impatient adult would do; I quit college to work there. I kind of regret it, but it happened. I never looked back and always had a job in graphics since 1991. I've only changed jobs four times since then, I have never been on disability, and I never got government help.

Years went by working, and I eventually got married to someone I had met in college. She was born deaf in one ear and partial hearing (with help from a hearing aid) in the other. I was less focused on being "crippled" because things were just so normal. We bought a townhouse soon after she got pregnant. The first thing I thought was, "I wonder if my daughter will have what one of us has?" At that time I was only aware I had some form of Cerebral Palsy, and my wife was hearing impaired. Take the fear of any new mom and dad wondering if the baby would be healthy, magnify that with two parents that had some issues, and you will understand my fear. I still had no other diagnosis, and was not aware I had Schizencephaly. Luckily things were fine. Our baby girl was born, with no problems, in 1998. After that I really forgot about what I was dealing with, and my attention was on my beautiful daughter.

Life was good for a while. After the birth of my daughter, I began a new chapter in life. Even though there were highs, there is always a drop somewhere. Not long after Tephanie's birth, my mother had a stroke while getting a catheter in her heart, and she lost her vision. That's when my stress began. As if that were not enough, we found out she had diabetes and had a lot of complications because of it. For years she had been fighting for me, and now the tables had turned. I was worried about her all the time, and now *I* was the one that had to push *her* to fight. My mother was always forcing me to be strong because she never saw me as a child that was different; I wanted to do the same for her. I realized it was my time to compose my strength into prayer and support. My dad had it very hard. He stayed by my mother's side every minute and took care of her. I was engulfed in worry and under a lot of stress, and my body was starting to feel it.

Years passed, and then my mother went into a diabetic coma. She was in the hospital on life support for a month or so. I used to go up to the hospital every day to sing to her and read her the Bible. Maybe I just believed she would be comforted by my voice and hear my appreciation for all those prayers in the dark she never knew I knew about.

One dreadful day, the doctors said she wasn't going to come back to us. Nothing prepares anyone for these days, and you go through a desperate moment of wanting to just have one more day, one more talk, one more chance to tell your mother you are so grateful for her tough love. We, as a family, made the very hard decision to take her off life support. As anyone knows, making these decisions is not only a spiritually and mentally draining one, but something you sit hours agonizing over. I made it just in time to see her off with the family when she passed. I fell on top of her bed, and wept and screamed. It was devastating. After the funeral I was a zombie and I didn't eat for days. Now I was the one saying prayers in the dark, asking God to care for my mother, as she was in His hands now.

One night I went to bed and had a huge grand mal seizure in my sleep. I woke up delirious and to a scared wife. I went to see doctors and they did tests. I was stubborn and didn't like doctors, so didn't follow up like I was supposed to.

A year later, my marriage began falling apart and brought major stress to my mind and overall well-being. I laid down for a nap one afternoon and had another grand mal seizure and was rushed to the hospital. At that time in my life I avoided doctors, but this continued to a point of having to face the facts; I needed an opinion. More seizures led to tests, MRI's, EEG's, sleep studies, and every other kind of test that they do. That's when I found out I had Schizencephaly, there were clefts and slits in my brain. I had no idea what they were talking about, but I wished mom was there to finally get an answer to what she had been wondering all these years.

I kept insisting I was this way because of Cerebral Palsy and lack of oxygen to the brain. They said "Yes, when you were born Cerebral Palsy could have been an issue, but your brain scan also shows you definitely have Schizencephaly."

I started seeing a neurologist regularly and started taking seizure medications. My first introduction to seizure meds was Depakote. Wow! What an adjustment there! I really noticed the side effects from that drug.

I began realizing the seizures changed me. My balance was badly thrown off, I had feelings of vertigo, and I spaced out to where I could see people talking, but I just stared with no emotion. I smiled on the outside, but felt raged madness on the inside. I leveled out somewhat, but still had waves of those effects for five years.

While all this going on, I was also going through a separation and got my own place and began adjusting to the single life. I also spent a lot of time looking for answers about what could be done for my condition. There was not much for me to go on except what little was known about Schizencephaly and its symptoms. As far as information, it just did not exist.

As time went on, I gave up. Then doctor took me off of Depakote, telling me it is a bad drug. Depakote is now known to cause pancreatic cancer, and was really bad for the liver. He decided to try Lamictal. I took that for a while, but I felt like it wasn't right for me. I wasn't myself, I was zombie-fied and used to wake up at night, and my limbs would lock up. I always had trouble sleeping. I lived in fear I was going to have a seizure while I was alone. That is the ugly side of this Schizencephaly; the unknown.

I had my appendix explode shortly after getting on medication and learning of my new diagnosis. I was still trying to wrap my head around what Schizencephaly was. Even the doctors were baffled. I was on bed rest for a couple months and realized I was losing my ability to walk. I had a rough year trying to regain my strength in my legs. I almost went on disability, but my stubborn self decided to defeat another obstacle. Nothing will get in my way when I am determined. I have learned when someone tells me I can't, I am even more fueled to do it and prove them wrong. I pushed through agonizing pain when I walked. I went to work and did my thing as usual, and got past that chapter.

Years later, the doctor decided to change meds again. I had to take two different medications at once; Lamictal and Keppra. That threw me through a loop, I was hallucinated big time. I thought there was a cat in my couch and tore the whole place apart looking for it. I had a chat with my doctor and he decided to try yet another medication.

A couple of years ago I began having more side effects, twitching being one of them. Along with these new symptoms was Tardive Dyskinesia in my jaw, wrist, and leg. Once again we changed medications. It was a little frustrating, but as someone with Schizencephaly, we have to get the right drug to control and adverse side effects. The doctor raised the dosage of Keppra, and I was finally getting better. I still had side effects, but not as bad.

I currently work as a graphic artist. I find all kinds of things to do to stimulate my brain. I enjoy learning new hobbies like painting, juggling sticks, ride bicycles, and swimming. I'm not sure what's next, but I know I'll take it on and move up to another level.

I recently started looking up Schizencephaly again because I am concerned with aging, and what I might have to face the older I get. There are lots of new treatments and new research that has happened, and I hope to find more. The more people know about Schizencephaly, the more that can be solved, and the more that people can overcome. All I know is; there is a voice in your head. It's God, and He has always been there, without fail. Listen to Him, and He will get you out of anything and lead you to a solution, a breakthrough of wisdom, when you let go and trust in Him. God is the one who kick-started me into my journey, and will push me forward into the future.

Although this story ends here for now, a new chapter is right around the corner.

Jennifer

When I was 22, I found out I was going to have another child, and a blessing to my little family. At 26 weeks gestation, Jay and I found out it was a girl. We were ecstatic! We also found out there may be issues. Our daughter was in a breech position, with her feet touching her head. The good news was the ultrasound was we were told that even with her being breech, everything looked great and we were having a healthy baby girl.

Although we expected some complications due to the baby's positioning, we felt confident that since the doctor caught it early, things would go smoothly once the delivering hospital got her into the right position.

On May 10, 2003, our precious baby was born and we named her Jennifer Michele. And what a beautiful girl she was. We thought the worst had passed, until we met some doctors with words that seemed to make time stop. Our baby, our special angel, could not hold down any fluids and needed to be rushed to the University of Tennessee's NICU. It was there we were told Jennifer had club feet, which (we were told) was due to her being breech, but we were assured her feet would straighten out.

The day Jennifer was born was the same day life changed for my family in an instant. It seemed that the longer we waited for answers, the more things began to get worse for Jen's prognosis. The staff ordered X-rays and we learned Jennifer's tummy was turned and she would need to be fed by an Nasojejunal tube (N-J tube).

We were still in the hospital when the doctor wanted yet another test. Jenn was two days old when a CT scan was ordered for her head to see how much damage was caused by a lack of oxygen. That was the day we found out we had a miracle because the CT scan showed two parts of the brain were missing.

Jennifer had Bilateral Open-Lip Schizencephaly, Arthrogryposis, Cerebral Palsy, Chronic Lung Disease, Epilepsy, Asthma, Tracheomalacia, and Scoliosis. We didn't know why this had happened, but we soon realized this was the beginning of our Jennifer's story. One that would teach my family how life is an ever changing ride, and we got our seat belts on for a long road.

The day Jennifer turned one month old; she went through a G-Tube placement, with the turning of her tummy, and a Nissen Fundoplication. We were told Jennifer wouldn't live six months and she would be a complete vegetable. We decided that home was the best place to be, and that we would fill her heart with all the love possible if she were to only be here a short while. We brought Jennifer home eight weeks after being placed in the NICU. We started corrective casting for the club feet, and splints on her hands.

It seemed Jen was just as much a fighter as any of us in this family. When Jennifer hit the six month mark, we celebrated because not only was she living, but she was holding her head up some. She still couldn't focus very well, but we went to church and the Pastor came to our pew, picked Jennifer up and carried her up and down the aisle praying over her. When the pastor brought her back to the pew, her eyes were focusing and not bouncing. GOD is good!

Jennifer had 30+ surgeries in her life, but always smiled. She was just so very happy to see the world and also to be loved and to share that love with everyone she met, but there were the bad days too. Jennifer spent her first two birthdays, Christmas', and Thanksgivings in the hospital from illness and surgeries. But when her third birthday came around, she had a big birthday party because she was actually spending her special day at home.

Jennifer started school at age three and she absolutely loved it. Her therapists and teachers had never had a child with so many disabilities or that needed to be G-Tube fed, but they quickly learned how to care for her. The friends she made and teachers that were touched by her proved she was a living angel.

By the time Jennifer went to school, she could sit up on her own and say momma. She shocked her doctors. The doctors were so amazed by Jennifer that they used her as a poster child. She was moving mountains even though she never walked. We received TEIS (Tennessee Early Intervention Services) and TIPS (Tennessee Infant Parent Services) that helped us with many referrals and transitions. Jennifer took occupational, physical, and speech therapy, which helped her a great deal, but she still couldn't eat by mouth. Speech helped us learn how to brush her teeth with her Arthrogryposis from limited jaw and joint movement.

It seemed Jennifer had a mission in this life. Even I as her mom never understood, but she was so very determined, and I could not have been any more proud. When Jennifer went kindergarten at age five, she was sitting, rolling from back to side, pointing out colors, and working on signing because she had a limited vocabulary. At this time she could say momma, bubby, paw, and no.

When she was six, Jennifer was going even further. She could sign, pick the right colors to color with, count on her left hand, and make the Letters J, N, T, and O, and she could draw straight lines and circles. She was excelling so much the teachers chose her as their helper.

There were so many miracles throughout Jennifer's life. She was determined to prove everyone wrong from day one, and I began to realize that no one can tell you what to expect from your child. Only God knows what the purpose of each of us in on this Earth, so in Him I trusted.

At the age of seven years, nine months, and 3 days, Jennifer got the flu. Late that night I went in to check on her, and her fever was high. I rushed to call the doctor. He assured me she would be fine, and to take her in the following morning. Later that day it seemed the flu was easing up. I was out when I got a call from Jay. It is something no mother is ever prepared for. We lost Jen and she was unresponsive. The ambulance took her to the hospital where she was revived, but our angel was in a coma and placed on Life Support. I was told she may not make it, and she needed to be airlifted to the

East Tennessee Children's Hospital.

On Valentine's Day, 2011, a nurse helped Jen's daddy dress her in a crown and earrings, and put her hair up in a ponytail. She laid there completely silent while we sat near making sure our princess looked just how she loved to look. The doctor came in and talked to Jay and I. We were told the next day they would do some test to determine if Jennifer would come out of her coma. If not, Jay and I had no choice in the matter of taking her off of support. That day seemed to be one of the longest, and shortest, I have ever been through.

On February 15th, 2011, at 4:33 P.M., my baby passed away. Words simply cannot express how that feels to anyone; to feel helpless, to live past your child. There is a hole that somehow never gets filled. Even though you learn to laugh again and life goes on, there are many days the pillow becomes your counselor.

I miss her laughter, her smile, her cuddles, and arguments with her brother and sister. I just miss Jen. I miss the smells, the routines you get used to. Sometimes a simple breeze carries a memory that brings me back to a good day, and can I see Jen's face smiling in the sunlight, so thankful to be who she was.

I know a lot of people would say how can I go on? I will tell you how; I get up every morning knowing I still have two beautiful children that loved Jen just as much as I, and a husband that needs me. I also find comfort from a support group and helping to raise awareness for Schizencephaly.

Jennifer is looking down on me. She is in all of my thoughts, and a part of all the families I meet that deal with Schizencephaly. When a child that is touched by Schizencephaly gets their wings, Jennifer is there waiting, smiling, and reaching out her hands to welcome them with all her love. Together they run and play and smile down on us.

On those days that you feel the warm sun briefly when the chilly wind stops for a moment; that is my Jen. She is reminding me that through the clouds there is always the light, and light fills the heart much faster than the dark.

TRICIA DENNIS and STEPHANIE ZIEMANN

Lily

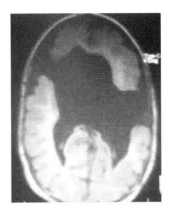

It was a typical Wednesday on June 25, 2009. I recently just moved back to Colorado, and I was living with my mom and step-dad. I came home from work, ate dinner, watched T.V. with my parents, and then went to bed. I woke up around 3 A.M. with back pain and abdominal cramps. It was around the time for me to start menstruating, so I didn't think much of it. I took Tylenol and plugged in my heat pad/ and went back to sleep. I called off work when I woke up later that morning. I also told my mom I wasn't feeling well and was staying home. My mother had meetings in Denver that day, about an hour and a half away, but wanted me to call if I needed anything. It was very unusual for me to be sick or miss work.

Around 9 A.M. I started to have a lot of lower pelvic pressure. My back was aching, and I felt like I had to urinate, but nothing would come out when I tried. As I was sitting on the toilet, I looked between my legs and I could see a finger with a strip of hair. I was having a baby! I had been on birth control, never felt any movement, no morning sickness, and my cycle was normal. There were no signs of pregnancy. I was in complete shock. I tore the shower curtain back, placed my hand on the wall, looked up at the ceiling, and thought, "Well, if I can see hair, the baby is ready and probably can't breathe." I stripped off my clothes and started to bear down. Her head came out and I cleared her airway with my fingers. Then she cried! My dogs came running down the hallway and into the bathroom. I was standing in the shower holding her head, overwhelmed and trying to get the dogs to quiet down. I pushed out the rest of her body. I obviously wasn't expecting this, so I didn't have a receiving blanket handy. I grabbed my t-shirt and wrapped her up. The whole time I was waiting for contractions to start and the worst imaginable pain of my life, but nothing was happening.

After about two minutes, I knew I need to cut the umbilical cord. I put a hand towel between my legs and carried her to the kitchen. I grabbed scissors, a zip lock bag, and some wash cloths. I then went back in the bathroom to cut the cord. I filled the sink with warm water and began to wash her off. Still no contractions, so I gently started pulling on the severed cord and the placenta came free. It was intact, and I placed it in the bag.

This entire time, Lily was bundled up on the floor mats while I cleaned up her, myself, and the bathroom. I noticed she wasn't staying very warm, so I stripped down and laid her skin to skin on my chest, and wrapped us in my robe while I text my mom. My mom was still in her meeting and I didn't want to alarm her, so I hadn't told her I just had a baby, just that she should call me as soon as possible. She said she would call me back in 10 minutes.

I was very calm throughout the entire process. My water never broke, there was very little amniotic fluid when Lily came out, I wasn't bleeding, and Lily was breathing evenly. I thought everything was going well, considering.

My mom called and I told her the news. She was laughing (I am quite the jokester). I got off the phone and sent her a picture message. She immediately called back and said, "I'm calling an ambulance. You are in shock!"

"Mom, I'm fine, the baby is fine, and I can't afford a $3,000 ambulance ride. When you get here you can take us to the hospital. If the baby starts having difficulties I'll call, but right now it's not an emergency." I said.

At this point, my Mom said; "Only you Jennifer!"

Lily was at 28 - 29 weeks gestation. They had to guess because I didn't know that I was pregnant, and had been having a regular cycle throughout my pregnancy. She was 14 inches long, and weighed 2 lbs. 9 oz. She was stabilized at our local hospital, but they didn't have a NICU, so she was then transported to The Children's Hospital in Aurora, near Denver, Colorado.

The team there was fantastic. Lily was doing very well considering how premature she was. During transport, Lily was intubated, but was breathing on her own within 12 hours. She presented as a typical preemie and nothing seemed unusual.

On the tenth day, they did an ultrasound to look for a bleed on Lily's brain. Bleeding on the brain sometimes happens with preemies. The images weren't very clear, and they ordered an MRI. That was when Lily was diagnosed with Bilateral Open-Lip Schizencephaly. I was told this was a very rare brain malformation, the umbrella term is Cerebral Palsy, and that they didn't really know why this happens or what her quality or longevity of life would be. She also was diagnosed with CVI (Cortical Visual Impairment), and Congenital Nystagmus.

When the attending neurologist went over Lily's MRI with my mother and I, it was very difficult to focus on exactly what she was saying. I distinctly remember her saying that Lily would more than likely suffer seizures, have severe motor delays, and have Cerebral Palsy with poor motor movement, plus vision and feeding problems.

I took it all in. I was already overwhelmed with being a mother unexpectedly, and then to hear this was just devastating. I asked if they knew which skills she would have difficulties developing with the areas of her brain missing. The neurologist said no, there really wasn't a way to know because sometimes other areas of the brain can take over and new pathways can be created. From that point on I refused to believe that my child would be a diagnosis or textbook. I remember going home that night and crying in my room for hours, questioning why this happened. Lily had fought so hard to be here, was this really how her life was going to be? It just wasn't fair.

The hospital had given me some pamphlets with random statistics showing that 1 out of 100,000 births resulted in Schizencephaly. Many children were immobile, on ventilators, ranged from mild to severe mental retardation, and were non-verbal. Basically, the worst case scenarios, and nothing dated within the last 15 years. Later that night I found only one support group, while looking for answers on my own online.

My mother and I went to Poudre Valley Hospital in Fort Collins, Colorado to get a second opinion. I had brought the written reports and CD with Lily's MRI results. This doctor was a personal and professional friend of my mother's, and we both wanted honest feedback on what to expect for Lily's quality of life, and what exactly her daily care would entail. I was very anxious to get any and all the information on Schizencephaly that I could.

The doctor started our meeting by expressing sorrow at Lily's profound diagnosis. She explained how physically, emotionally, and mentally exhausting it may be to provide care for my daughter. Then she gave me information on signing over my rights and open adoption. I had thought about adoption before receiving Lily's diagnosis because obviously she wasn't planned, but this was all so surreal. With all the unknowns and infinite possibilities for her life, I knew that I couldn't just walk away and entrust her care to someone else.

While Lily was in the NICU at the Children's Hospital, I had been meeting with all of the service coordinators that I could to make sure that she would receive the maximum amount of therapies as soon as we were home.

I could not wait for Lily to be able to come home. Going back and forth from home to the hospital was hard. I rarely slept while I was at the hospital. Her alarms were going off every time her heart rate would jump up. And there were hearing tests, vision tests, neurologists, physical therapists, lactation specialists, and the list goes on and on. Lily was so tolerant of everything, and her nurses kept telling me that she didn't present as most neurologically deficient babies did. Lily spent 53 days in the NICU, and was home almost a month sooner than they led me to be believe she would be.

Lily came home on 1 Liter of oxygen for a mandatory 30 days because of our elevation here in Denver, and her being premature. There was also a multivitamin supplement that she took orally with her bottle feedings. Lily had been healthy, and we had been fortunate to not have many issues besides acid reflux and aspiration. Later on, she started having seizures.

Early Intervention provided physical, occupational, and speech therapists that I got to interview and select to come to my home to work with Lily. Lily struggled to open her hands, track anything visually, hold her head up, and drink from a bottle. She would also get extremely congested. I was constantly suctioning her nose, and running a vaporizer.

Eating was also a struggle. Every moment that she was awake I spent trying to feed her just to keep her hydrated. She was burning more calories trying to eat than she was storing. For every 6 ounces Lily drank, she threw up 5. Then she would be asleep for 40 minutes and wake up starving. This didn't happen with every feed, but the vomiting usually happened three times a day.

Her therapists and I made light boxes for her to lay in, utilized pinwheels, bells, any crackly sounding or reflective materials, and kinesiology tape. We did color therapy, sound therapy, and aromatherapy. I used exfoliating gloves to "dry rub" all over Lily's body to increase body awareness and increase blood flow. We also did side laying with correct body alignment to encourage mid-line play, and strengthening positions. All this was done on top of watching for seizure activity.

I spent most of my time doing Lily's therapies and stressing about paying my bills. Looking back, I don't know how we made it through those days! Schizencephaly is already a big scary sounding word. Coupled with all these specialists telling you they don't really know that much about it, it is terrifying! And I learned this was something I must tackle head on since the health word seemed baffled.

Lily's biological father has never seen her or expressed the desire to understand what we go through on a daily basis. Without the support of my mom, step-dad, and boyfriend, I don't know how I would have been able to make it through the very hard first months.

I am a strong person, and have always been very optimistic and positive about Lily. I have tried my hardest to be the best advocate for her and make sure she has every opportunity to experience life. The hardest decision I have had to make for her was a surgical procedure. It took me 23 months to go forward with a G-tube placement and Nissen Fundoplication. I was spending 9 to 11 hours a day feeding her. Lily wouldn't sleep for longer than four hours at a time. I was going to school to become a CNA, and then she started having seizures. I was worried that with the reflux she wasn't retaining her seizure medicine. Lily was also not gaining weight. In my mind, if you aren't getting the correct nutrition, your development mentally and physically is affected. Sleep patterns and you're temperament suffer. Lily deserved better than me just cleaning up her vomit and trying to feed her as much as possible the next time she had the strength to eat. I felt like a complete failure, I mean what kind of mother can't feed her own child?! I so desperately wanted her to one day just be able to drink from a bottle safely, and to be able to have some "normalcy".

Now though, I see her smiling, laughing, exploring the world, and being so much more engaged. I truly wish I would've had this procedure done sooner. We still work on introducing foods to her every day with different textures with purees and thickened nectar. We're currently working on using straws and blowing bubbles.

In December 2010, previous to her G-tube being placed, she had Strabismus surgery. Lily's eyes, especially her left one, were constantly turned in. This surgery cut the muscles in the inner eye so that they would no longer cross, making her eyes sit level. The ophthalmologist held the dye up to my eye so that I could see the degree that her eyes were turned. There is no possible way she could have focused on anything, near or far! Just try it. Cross your eyes and try to focus on something, and then move your head. It Gives me a headache just thinking about that day.

Lily had a bad reaction to the anesthesia and stopped breathing several times, but made it through. Lily had blood shot eyes for several days, but within a week I noticed her nystagmus (eyes shaking) diminishing. I felt she was able to track more effectively, neck strength increased, and there was improvement in her balance while she was supported sitting and doing tummy time.

Both of these procedures were done to improve the quality of her life, but were not medically necessary. I can't help but feel that if my daughter was able to vocalize exactly how she felt, or explain how she understands her environment, that she would get better treatment. It is a terrible feeling to doubt everything you are doing. Is my daughter happy? Yes I think she is. It is evident in the sound of her laughter when being tickled, played with, or talked to by her siblings. In her beautiful smile or her sounds of distress when you walk away from her, or when she reaches out and touches something that she wasn't expecting or didn't know was there. When we go places and she hears a new voice or feels the rain and wind on her face. Lily loves her life because she knows nothing else. I only hope she will always be so pure and happy. That is what I strive to provide for her every day.

Even though I knew that Lily was at risk to have seizures, it was so emotionally overwhelming when the first one happened. There is no amount of knowledge that can prepare you for seeing your child seizing. It is truly like they are just gone. Lily gets irritable usually about an hour before actively seizing. We have Diastat as a rescue medicine for her that needs to be administered if she has more than six seizures in an hour, or seizes for more than three minutes.

Theoretically, Diastat is supposed to immediately make her stop seizing. That is not however always the case. Usually within two minutes of administering, she stops seizing. On January 31, 2012, she ended up seizing for 90 minutes, and stopped breathing for 15 minutes, resulting in her being bagged and developing pneumonia. Lily was hospitalized for three nights.

I am able to handle her mental and physical delays, and everything that goes along with her care, but the seizures I struggle with. There is no way to know what will trigger them or how deeply she'll seize. I also struggle to deal with the reality that her little body may not be able to tolerate the uncontrollable firing in her brain, and that seizures might take her life. I absolutely HATE seizures.

I am so fortunate to have the support of my mother and my boyfriend's mother. They are both willing and able to help in watching our other children while Lily has been hospitalized, when I have errands or need to go grocery shopping, and of course, to allow Kyle and I date nights. Our family is also very close, supportive, and understanding of all Lily's doctor appointments and therapies.

Our other children are five years, 18 months, and four months old. I have discussed with Lily's primary physician getting respite care for her when our lives get busier with sports or other extracurricular activities, and trips that Lily may not be able to attend due to travel restrictions, her inability to filter environment changes such as heat, new schedules, sensory overload (which involves more breakthrough seizures), the inevitable emergency, and being away from her very involved and competent medical team. These decisions will be made with the happiness of our whole family, but I haven't been able to come to terms yet with having family outings without her. We try to stay within 90 minutes of home and have found many good places that accommodate our entire family.

Lily is the number one priority in my life. She has taught me patience, self-worth, persistence, hard work, empathy, compassion, true vision, trust, and unconditional love. Our path in life hasn't been the easiest, but I believe that no path in life is ever easy. Growing up I often heard, "You get what you get, and you don't throw a fit." I apply this to my life every single day, in many contexts.

I am so thankful for all of the abilities that I have. Opening my eyes looking at the alarm clock, getting out of bed, bathing myself, walking to the closet to pick out my clothes for the day, brushing my teeth, making myself breakfast, telling my family members that I love them; whether it is with words, a hug, picking them up, or just making eye contact. Lily functions on the level of a six month old developmentally, but will be three years old in June. Her smile is so infectious, and her laugh just makes my heart want to burst. With the challenges she faces, she almost always has a smile on her sweet face. She never says, "No, that's too hard," or "I can't do that."

My daughter is truly my miracle and I love her dearly. I can't think of one person that doesn't love interacting with her. All of her doctors, therapists, family members, and our friends are continuously amazed at how expressive she is vocally. Even though she is non-verbal or animated, her facial expressions are! Every moment with Lily is truly a blessing. I feel that being the mother to a child with special needs has made me a better person.

Lily does not sit independently, crawl or walk; she is non-verbal, legally blind and has a seizure disorder. Lily has received occupational, speech, physical, and vision therapies from birth four times a week. She has AFO's for her hands, and her feet need to be recast every six to nine months. She has a stander that she is in for a minimum of three hours every day. A bath chair and a special car seat to offer her the support she needs.

Our road has its challenges, but I never once considered my daughter a diagnosis or textbook. She is full of life and lives every moment to the fullest with absolute joy. I feel so fortunate to be her mother, advocate, and care giver. Yes it is tough, but geez, being a GOOD parent is tough!

Our children's needs should not be so hard to have met. Lily will be turning three in June. Thankfully I haven't had to deal with too much yet, but I know the future holds many debates on what her needs are. Lily will be transitioning to preschool this fall. I am in the process of establishing directives for the school nurse and arranging her therapies. I have been trying to get them all together since January; we have finally set a date for May 9th. She was fit for a wheelchair in January, and should be receiving that in the next two months or so.

My daughter is on Medicaid, and while I am very thankful, it is extremely frustrating the amount of redundant paper work involved in the approval process for adaptive equipment. Sometimes I feel like Lily and her needs are just a number, and that the financial burden she places on the government for her care is more important than the care itself. I feel the government is trying to safeguard disability funds when maybe they should be restricting other areas of spending.

Lily will also be having Femoral Derotational Osteotomy Surgery this summer on both of her femurs to keep the head of her femur in her hip. Right now she is 80% subluxated, meaning very close to dislocation. The muscles are constantly contracting, so when she tries to take a step, her hamstring and abductors shorten, pulling her foot across the front of her knee and along the opposite side of her weight bearing foot, also known as "scissoring." This is an invasive surgery, but we are confident that it will improve the quality of her life now, and hopefully minimize, if not eliminate, any future hip issues.

This year we have seen many improvements in Lily's spatial awareness, social interactions, strength, balance, and coordination. We are continuously trying to find creative ways to stimulate her and teach others how to interact with her. She loves watching and listening to Sprout Network cartoons, all types of music, using her iPad, being a plane throughout the house while I describe what room we're in and what's on the walls, being tickled, and loved with kisses and hugs.

Lily is absolutely everything to me, and I couldn't imagine my life without her in it!

TRICIA DENNIS and STEPHANIE ZIEMANN

Andrew

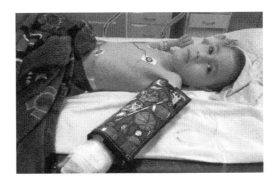

When my husband and I started doing foster care in 2001, I only wanted to take behaviorally challenged children. I had worked with many children with various behavior problems and felt confident that we would be able to be good parents to those types of children. What I didn't want was a child with physical or cognitive issues because, quite honestly, they scared me. I didn't know what to do with them.

Eight and a half years, ten boys, and three adoptions later, I was invited to go to my neighbor's to see her latest addition, a very tiny baby boy born with a rare brain condition called Schizencephaly. He was only six days old, and had already lost two families. His birth family placed him up for adoption prior to his birth, and an adoptive family backed out when they found out about his brain disorder.

My neighbor was also a foster mother, but she had specialized in medically fragile infants. She was often called to the hospital to pick up newborns; such was the case with this child. We had taken one of her babies once before in the hopes of adopting him, but it hadn't worked out, and I think she was hopeful that we'd consider this child. I knew that that would not be the case. Obviously God intended for me to take older boys, and a baby was not in my future.

Besides, we all knew that the problems this child would face were way beyond anything I was familiar with.

Holding him that day, I told him so. I told him I would love to come play with him, but only until he found his home. I had four other active boys at home and I didn't have time for a baby, especially one who would have long term issues. And yet I found myself as his perspective adoptive mother two weeks later at his first neurology appointment.

"Don't take this child, he has Schizencephaly. He is likely going to be deaf, blind, unable to speak or eat, plagued by seizures, paralyzed, and cognitively impaired. You really don't want him. You'd be better off to walk away. No one would blame you."

Those were the words the neurologist told me as I sat there holding that tiny, helpless child; the one who had already been rejected twice. They confirmed what little information I had been able to locate on Schizencephaly through my own research. The prognosis was grim. The neurologist admitted to not knowing much about Schizencephaly, and that she'd been trying to find information for us. She didn't have his MRI to look at, but showed us pictures in medical books of other children's MRIs. The pictures painted a very bleak future for the beautiful little boy in my arms.

We left the office, and it was a pretty quiet ride back to where we had left my truck when we'd met up before the appointment. When she dropped me off, I told my friend and neighbor, "I guess that's that". I was totally overwhelmed. After all, the child I thought I wanted was going to be everything I knew I didn't, I didn't have to take him. I had four boys at home; three boys we'd already adopted, and one we were in the process of adopting, all of which fit my original plans. If I wanted more boys, they were fairly easy to come by as "foster care" and "behavior problems" pretty much go hand in hand. The neurologist was right, I should just walk away.

Laying in bed that night, after filling my husband in on everything the neurologist had to say and making every argument possible to back up the decision not to take the baby, I couldn't sleep. I kept thinking about that little baby and prayed to God for direction. Eventually I told my husband that the neurologist was wrong- I did want that little boy. He agreed, and I called my neighbor the next morning. She said that she knew I'd come around and asked what I wanted to name him. Andrew Ryan moved in six months later and changed our lives forever.

The last three and a half years have been quite the journey. I've had to learn a whole new language in order to understand the doctors and therapists when it comes to the treatment of my son. For the first two years, every cold meant breathing treatments. Even now, every fever means a trip to the ER. He has had a second MRI, three VEEG's, and countless X-ray's and blood draws. He had his first, and so far only, seizure this past Christmas. He still cannot sit, stand, crawl, or walk by himself. He can't feed himself or even hold his own bottle, which is still required three times a day in order to meet his daily calorie requirement even though he will be four years old soon. He wears glasses, AFO's, and hand splints for part of each day. His equipment includes things such as a wheelchair, gait trainer, Hart walker, and an activity chair. He has multiple therapists and specialists. It takes hours just to coordinate his care, and I drive at least a thousand miles a week, most of which is for him. I've learned to navigate the world of hospitals, therapy centers, and IEP's on a whole new level, and I spend more time with therapists than with friends.

Life with my son is a blessing, not a burden. He has proven the neurologist wrong so many times. He can see. He can hear. He is considered nonverbal, but is learning how to use a communication device and a computer that is adapted with switches. He does say several words, "mom" being his first and my favorite. He is learning to commando crawl and has started rolling over. He walks with the help of his equipment and will even be able to play soccer this summer and baseball next spring. He loves horseback riding and to watch the horse races. I think that when he watches the horses running, he can imagine what it would feel like to run so fast. He is highly intelligent and empathic beyond his years. He is his brothers' biggest fan, and loves to watch their games.

Andrew has beaten the odds time and time again. He works harder, without complaining, than anyone I've ever known. We have learned to celebrate the small things and not to worry about the big milestones he may never reach. He has taught our little community how to come together and work for a common goal, and that it is the journey that matters, not the destination. Andrew is a social little guy whose smile can and has melted the hardest of hearts. He is a child nobody wanted. He chose me, and I'm so blessed he calls me mom.

TRICIA DENNIS and STEPHANIE ZIEMANN

Rafe

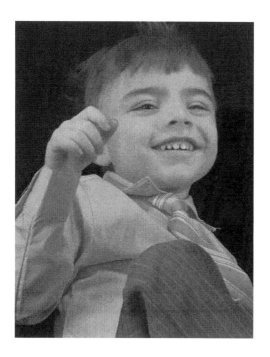

To tell this story requires me to look into the past. Looking back allows us to see where we have been, no matter how painful. "Special needs" are two words I have known practically all my life. My younger sister was born with Spina Bifida, and watching her grow up has taught me so much. I never knew just how many valuable things I had learned until I met my beautiful and stubborn son, Rafe.

My water broke early on March 1, 2009. I was so excited that our little boy was getting ready to make his arrival. We headed to labor and delivery, which is totally different in Wiesbaden, Germany. The doctors don't explain anything to you; they just do what they have to do. .

I was put on Pitocin at 10 A.M. to help start my contractions. After six hours of fun and progress I was ready to push, and Rafe Liam Thomas was born at 4:20 P.M. I was so exhausted that I didn't realize my main blood vessel was torn when Rafe made his appearance and had lost a lot of blood. Rafe had excellent scores after birth, he received 9's and 10's, and we were proud of him.

I spent the next 24 hours bonding with Rafe, and being in

disbelief that he was really here. Rafe was periodically taken back to the nursery for a blood sugar check and was taken back for his second check in the early morning hours on March 3. The nurse told me to get some sleep and they would wake me when he was done.

I was woken in a rush at 5 A.M. by the head doctor of the Neonatal Intensive Care Unit at my bedside telling me that Rafe was having seizures and was rushed to the NICU. I was so lightheaded that I thought it was a dream. She told me the information a second time and I started throwing up so much that they knocked me out.

When I woke up again it was 11 A.M. I was frantic to see my son and know how he was doing. After the nurse told me where the NICU was, I slowly got out of bed and went to the elevators with the worst thoughts running through my head. I got down to the door of the NICU and rang the bell. I had to wait 20 minutes to see him, and was in tears by the time I got through the hand washing and into a gown and mask. The staff inside the NICU barely spoke English, but I finally found Rafe in a room all hooked up to needles and wires. I grabbed the chair for support and just let the tears run down my face.

I will never forget the first seizure I saw; only the left side of Rafe's little body moved. The nurse came running in and told me that Rafe had had over 100 seizures since arriving in the NICU. I could only cry and nod my head. I was able to reach in and touch his body with my fingers and watch the tears fall down his face. There was nothing I could do but cry with him as I waited for the doctor to come in and give me Rafe's diagnosis.

I cannot describe how much my heart broke hearing what the doctor told me that day, I was even more astounded by what she didn't tell me. She could barely speak English, all she told me that Rafe had a very rare disorder called Schizencephaly and that she was sorry, then handed me papers she had gotten from a colleague from Belgium.

I quickly read the papers and my whole world fell apart in an instant. I learned that Rafe was missing a large portion of the right side of his brain. I never felt more alone in my life than that moment. I couldn't read any more, I could only cry. I cried for my son who was struggling to live, I cried for what I had just lost, and most of all, I cried for my husband and son who had no idea of what was coming.

I headed back up to my room and tried to stop the tears. When I saw my oldest son, I knew I couldn't speak any words. I handed my husband the papers and cried myself to sleep in the bed next to my son, Gregory.

The next day passed in a daze. I was released from the hospital, and it broke my heart to leave Rafe. I watched Gregory cry and wish he could help his brother. I couldn't believe this was happening, and I cried the whole way home. I knew I couldn't continue this way so I began to research his disorder, trying to find anything that would help Rafe.

My husband and I took turns visiting Rafe each day so he would never have to be alone. I held him each night and told him how much we all loved him. After 14 days, he became stable enough to go home and I was beyond excited. Before we got to go home, we were told how dim Rafe's future looked. He wouldn't be able to walk, talk, or do much of anything. He was started on Phenobarbital, and would always need to be on medications to control the seizures. I was scared and wondered how I was ever going to through this. I was also sad that Rafe had been through so much already, and it was only the beginning.

I worried about every movement and cry I heard. Rafe slept so much the first few months, but when he was awake he would smile when he heard my voice and laugh when I tickled him. I cried tears of happiness at his smiles and laughter. These moments of normalcy gave me hope and the strength to get out of bed in the morning.

When Rafe was three months old we transitioned to a new seizure medicine, and it was torturous. He cried so much that first week, it was heart breaking. After we made it through that hurdle, Rafe was awake more and I began to see his personality. Rafe is happy, and I mean truly happy. He always has a smile on his face and love in his eyes. It is his bright, ever-loving personality that got me through the next couple months while my husband was deployed.

In January of 2010, I took Rafe to have his eyes checked because he wasn't tracking like he should be. I hated taking Rafe to the eye doctor since they had to look in his eyes and Rafe always cried so much. The doctor came in and had a translator with him to tell me that had bad news; my child was essentially blind and would never see. I was in shock when he told me had bad news, I never for the life of me thought he would say those words. I was mad, upset, and angry at what was happening. Here I was by myself, again, and I had to give my husband more bad news.

My husband came home on emergency leave so we could visit an American eye doctor. We were told that Rafe could see, but they couldn't tell what he was able to see due to the cleft in his brain, and he would most likely be declared legally blind. We were upset, and this was the second time I had seen my husband cry. We decided it was time to talk about moving back to the States where we could get better care for Rafe.

In February 2010, we took Rafe to a routine neurologist appointment and he had his first seizure outbreak since birth. We were immediately admitted to the hospital and had an EGG to confirm seizures. I tried to mentally prepare myself for what would happen the following weeks, but I couldn't have prepared for it no matter how hard I tried, and began to cry.

Rafe was in the hospital over his first birthday, and was put on two medicines that made him extremely sick and pale. The American neurologist was concerned and wanted us to be transferred on base immediately instead of being at the German hospital. After we were transferred, we found out that Rafe had Hydrocephalus and would need immediate surgery to place a shunt to drain the fluid. However, we would have to go to another hospital that was 45 minutes away via ambulance. I was numb and decided that I had to be strong for my son. We were admitted to the hospital later that week, and started an eight week stay in Homburg, Germany.

Rafe had his first surgery March 22, 2010. They placed a regular shunt, which didn't work, and he had a programmable shunt placed

April 4, 2010. I watched Rafe cry, scream, and sleep days away. Eventually Rafe made a big come back and I got to see him smile and laugh once more.

It was a huge fight to get clearance to fly back to the States. Rafe was healing from the surgery, but his seizures were only increasing from 40 to 80 seizures a day. It was heartbreaking to watch, and being in Europe and getting mixed information was exhausting. The language barrier was very painful and caused us many sleepless nights. We were finally given clearance to leave and were back in the states by May 2010.

We tried desperately to get the seizures under control with medication after medication. Rafe would throw up and his weight dropped, and I was trying to hold it together for everyone else. The seizures got so bad that Rafe developed scoliosis, but his physical therapist was able to use Kinesiology Tape to help his scoliosis get better.

We have had to fight with the military insurance for a stander to help our son stand. We got Rafe a pony walker, and I cried tears of happiness when Rafe took his first steps. The doctors had told us Rafe would never walk, but he did it with a smile on his face!

Our biggest battle was with insurance to help with Rafe's seizures; they just would not pay for the surgeries he needed. Rafe had already been having seizures for three years, I was not about to let him suffer any more. He had his third surgery to implant the Vagus Nerve Stimulator (VNS) in November 2011, but caught Scarlett Fever three weeks later and ended up having it removed. We fought hard to find another doctor to put it back in. Rafe had surgery that February, and they were able to successfully re-implant the VNS.

Rafe recovered well and is happy. His ability to love and be happy brings smiles to my heart to this day. His stubborn nature will not allow him to give up, and neither will I. He has done what other people told us was impossible. He sits, he has walked, and he said his first word; Dada. Rafe has taught me the most important things; to never give up, and to live life to its fullest. To Rafe, nothing is impossible, and I will never stop believing that even little boys can reach out and touch the stars.

TRICIA DENNIS and STEPHANIE ZIEMANN

Yanni

My journey with my daughter, Yanni, began when she was born in December of 2001. I had a standard scheduled cesarean section. Surgery went wonderfully, and Yanni weighed in at a beautiful and healthy 7 pounds 8 ounces.

Right after birth, Yanni's blood sugar and oxygen saturation levels dropped, and the doctors couldn't figure out why. They placed her in the NICU for four days until they believed she was stable enough to send us home. I couldn't have been happier because, although Yanni hit that initial speed bump, she seemed to have come through just fine. She ate very well and behaved like any newborn would.

As time went by, I noticed that Yanni didn't seem like she was able to see very well. She wasn't tracking objects, and her eyes were bouncing around a lot. I brought it to the attention of our pediatrician at the time, and she blew it off as normal newborn behavior. I listened to her in the beginning, trying to disregard my gut feeling that something wasn't right.

In the meantime, Yanni developed a nasty case of Respiratory

Syncytial Virus (RSV), and we were again thrown into a state of complete worry as she fought for her life in the hospital. She became so weak that members of my family and my few close friends believed (though they didn't share these thoughts with me at the time) that Yanni might not pull through. By the grace of God, she did and we were sent home. I was relieved to have my little girl back in my arms and away from the hospital, doctors, and all of those beeping machines.

At Yanni's three month checkup, I brought up my concerns about her eyesight to the doctor and was again shot down and told not to worry. This time I decided it was time to seek the opinion of another pediatrician. I changed to a new doctor, and it was with her help that Yanni's diagnosis came to light.

We were sent by our new pediatrician to an ophthalmologist at Riley Children's Hospital Outpatient Center, in Indianapolis. After a very thorough evaluation of Yanni's eyes, the doctor determined that she had underdeveloped optic nerves and Nystagmus, and that these conditions were the cause of her vision issues. The doctor also ordered an MRI with contrast, based on her knowledge that generally children with underdeveloped optic nerves (or Optic Nerve Hypoplasia) may also have other latent issues with the brain.

One week later we traveled down to Riley Children's Hospital for Yanni's MRI. My little baby looked even tinnier than usual, laying so still on that long table with the machine whirling around her little head. The noise didn't seem to disturb her much, but it was really unnerving to me. I think I somehow knew I was stepping into a world where, for the first time, I would really be alone.

An appointment was immediately set for us to meet with the ophthalmologist, and that's where the doom and gloom predictions began. She basically said, in a nutshell, that my child had a disorder of the brain called Schizencephaly. Specifically, Yanni was diagnosed with Bilateral Open-Lip Schizencephaly. She added that it was very rare and little was really known or understood about the disorder, and that the majority of children with this disorder are severely disabled. My child would probably never walk, talk, or do any of the things a "normal" child might do. This was based not only on her diagnosis, but also on her MRI films that showed very large clefts, especially to the left side of her brain. I left that appointment absolutely devastated. My baby's future was uncertain, and I knew our lives would never be the same.

We were in Indianapolis the following week meeting with the doctor who would be Yanni's neurologist and things started to look up. The neurologist had done some genetic research and had several patients with Schizencephaly. He immediately put me at ease by explaining that children with this disorder generally present symptoms on a spectrum that can range from very mild to very severe. That the brain is a highly resilient organ, and often times it will make new pathways and connections to make up for any deficits. He showed me Yanni's films and said that they believe Schizence-phaly is caused by a problem that occurs sometime during the embryonic stage, when the neural tube forms, and cells that are meant to become the brain begin migrating up the tube, heading for their destinations. They believe that some malfunction happens and the cells that should migrate to this area or that area, for some unknown reason do not, and that is what causes the tell-tale clefts that help to define the disorder.

What stands out most in my memory is that he said, very succinctly, that he can't predict what Yanni will or will not do. Our job is to get her as far as she can go, one day at a time. I found a lot of hope in his words, and that's what I clung onto. I'm telling you all of this from memory, so of course it's not as eloquent as the doctor put it, but I'm repeating this because it was a lifeline for me. It was a beginning of understanding so to speak. The neurologist did an awesome job that day of making me believe that no matter what, we would be OK.

Since the day we learned Yanni's diagnoses, we've had plenty of speed bumps. Yanni was additionally diagnosed with Panhypopituitarism, and sees an endocrinologist for hormonal deficiencies. She is legally blind, and began having seizures last year. She's also been hospitalized for a number of illnesses including strep throat, a staph infection (she caught at the beach of all places), and an infected tick bite (even the back yard isn't safe). Yanni became underweight, and I had to make the very tough decision to have a G-tube placed into her belly to help supplement her diet – and this is a kid that really enjoys eating.

Despite all of this, I can say that Yanni is the strongest little girl I know, and she is always smiling. Her smile is the first thing people notice about her, and it is the one thing no one ever forgets. She has been the sunshine of our family, and she is the light in the lives of everyone she meets. Yanni loves to dance, read (she knows some sight words), playing with dollies, calling friends on her cell phone, tease and play with her sisters, and to snuggle with me when she has the chance. It's kind of hard sharing mom with four siblings, but Yanni takes it all in stride. She loves going to school, and she adores her teachers and her friends. She's very caring and loving toward others, and she adores little babies and animals. One of the most endearing qualities about my baby girl is that she absolutely loves The Beatles, and will sing all of their songs off key and two beats behind. Yanni likes to sing loud and proud.

I consider myself fortunate to be blessed with Yanni. She proves to me that even though we're walking a road that requires us to face some of the hardest of life's trials, you can be happy. She proves to me that strength comes in the smallest of packages. I've seen this kid stick out her arm for a shot that would make her 6 foot tall, 200 pound older brother weak in the knees. Yanni has taught me patience, kindness, and to appreciate the smallest of things. I am proud when I hear her say, "Mom, I love you."

I remember the first day I received Yanni's diagnosis, and I am grateful. I'm so glad that doctor was wrong, and that I heard those words about resilience from the neurologist. The brain is resilient. And our lives are definitely resilient if we remember to take it the only way we really can; one day at a time.

SCHIZENCEPHALY: ANGELS WITH BROKEN WINGS

TRICIA DENNIS and STEPHANIE ZIEMANN

Carrol

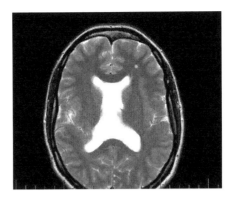

I'm told that as a baby I did the normal things that a baby should do, it wasn't until I was two years old that things started to change. At first it was minor things, like my left eye started to turn in. My optometrist said it was a lazy eye, and it ended up correcting itself by the time I was 10.

When I was in elementary school I couldn't run, jump, or hop on one foot very well. In my old school report cards teachers noted that I was not paying attention, I would stare off into space and miss instructions. My neurologist now says I was indeed having absence seizures as a child, and I continue to have them to this day.

Growing up, buying shoes for me was always a challenge because my left foot is one size smaller than my right. The neurologist measured me, and the entire left side of my body is smaller than my right.

I've always had slight hearing problems in my left ear, but was told there was nothing to worry about. I have 10% deafness in my left ear even though my ear works perfectly fine, I'm slightly hard of hearing because the connection from my ear to my brain is disrupted.

When I was 14, my face started to feel numb at odd times. I would feel weird and wouldn't be able to speak. Then I started to have fainting spells at school. I had no clue what was happening, and they were frightening. The numbness and fainting went on for many years and were brushed off as stress or anxiety. I have since found out that I was having seizures.

It wasn't until 2007 that I was actually diagnosed. I was living in Edmonton, Alberta, and my family was in the process of moving to Ontario. My fainting spells were getting worse. I often had an upset stomach, headaches, and would faint at work. This was all typical seizure activity, but I didn't know that that was what had been happening to me. My doctor sent me to have an MRI, and the cause for my symptoms was finally discovered.

The doctor told me that I had Schizencephaly. He explained the gist of the disorder to me and said I needed to see a neurologist to get further details. I left there in tears and feeling very alone. I was unsure what to think, but at least I finally had some answers to my 20 year long journey.

I researched Schizencephaly as much as I could when I got home. I read that there were very few adult survivors, and that made me feel even more alone and angry at the world.

I put my disorder on hold because of the move, and continued to call the fainting spells "episodes" so that no one would suspect anything. Once we moved to Ontario and settled in, I got a job and was feeling pretty good. The fainting spells would come in little spurts and then I wouldn't have any for a while, so I tried to forget about them.

In the summer of 2008, I found out I was expecting my fourth child. I ended up being in hospital nine times because I was vomiting nonstop. They did two blood transfusions which almost caused me to lose the baby. It was a horrible experience when they had to deliver her a month early due to my high blood pressure.

After giving birth I thought I could finally recover and move on with my life, but it all got worse, and things would never be the same again. I started having episodes every day; up to 25 a day. One day I was rushed to the hospital because I had collapsed to the ground. The hospital told me I had a mini-stroke and seizures. I wasn't having just one type of seizure; I was having five different types of seizures.

The seizures eventually became so bad that I had my license taken away. I would visit my neurologist once a month and go through tests, medications, and changes in medications; but I kept getting worse. My world was falling apart all around me, and I began to isolate myself. There was no one that I knew of who had what I had, no one that would understand what was happening to me, no one I could talk to. I thought what I was feeling and going through would make the people around me think I was crazy.

I was sent to Montreal, Quebec to be seen a neurosurgeon and his team of six other doctors to see if I was a candidate for surgery to try and stop these seizures. Unfortunately I was not a candidate, and there was nothing anyone could do.

They told me, "You will die as soon as we open you up if we

were to try and remove any part of your brain that is damaged. And if you don't die on the operating table, you will come out a vegetable because your brain has rewired itself and has used up all of its reserve to function properly."

If only I had known about my condition when I was younger and had been able to have gone to them sooner, maybe I would have had more of a chance of survival because my brain could have rewired itself after the surgery. The neurologist said that any adult that he has treated only lived for so long because of surgery.

He proceeded to say I shouldn't have children because the pushing of the baby's body on my body would be too hard on me. When I told him I had already given birth to four children, he turned to me and said, "You're considered a miracle. I would like to have permission to use your MRI to teach my students. Your brain is so complex because of all six of the clefts and slits, and the grey matter. When I read all the reports and scans, I would have not expected to have you walk in my office."

I suffer from severe seizures and migraines all the time. It is the part of this disorder many kids cannot talk about or express to their parents. Seizures are one of the ugliest sides of this disorder. I want to really explain what a seizure feels like so others can understand.

The symptoms vary with every seizure. My worst seizures, and the ones that I feel the most during, are what I call a "drop down". It begins by my entire body feeling like it's trembling, and then I lose control of my body. Next, I feel a sensation of cold wind blowing against my skin, my heart pounds so hard it feels like it's going to come through my chest. I sweat, I get a metallic taste in my mouth, my lips go numb, and then my tongue goes numb. I feel a sense of impending death and get very short winded. These symptoms are my forewarning.

Several minutes later I will feel like there is sudden jolt of electricity that will shoot from my feet to the top of my head. The left side of my face will go completely numb, and it feels like I have hair on my face. The numbness travels all the way down my arm. I will immediately look for someone as I feel myself collapsing. Suddenly, I am unable to make my arms or legs work. I am fully aware, but unable to speak because my jaw is usually tightly closed. I know what I want to say, and I can say it to myself in my mind, but I can't mouth the words. When the seizure finally takes ahold of all of me, it feels like a ton of bricks pushing on my chest, and it takes my breath away. Finally, I black out. I do not know what actually happens when I black out because normally no one is with me.

In one incident though, I came to momentarily. I saw my cat and noticed how huge his eyes were, but everything else was black. I argued with the cat that I could not move, and he insisted that I could. All these weird thoughts suddenly started to go through my mind. I began to call for my daughter (who was already sitting with me). I remember thinking, "Please don't touch me (touching me makes me feel agitated), but stay with me." I was trying to reach for my daughter, but could not do it. Things went black again. And then, just like that, I came back. My whole body felt very heavy, I was shaky and freezing, and I was in pain. Those feelings will last for the next three days.

My husband says I stare off to the right, blinking repeatedly, and my hands have a slight twitch when I have a seizure. He calls my name and I sometimes look towards him, but then my eyes blink and I look back up to the right. I breathe short breaths, and I sometimes drool. In a different type of seizure I will just sit, unable to move, but stare straight ahead and rock back and forth uncontrollably. My husband has also seen me walking and all of a sudden I go down like a wet noodle, and I wake up tired and cold.

Sometimes I can tell a seizure is coming and can call for someone or have time to brace myself until the episode passes, but I am still terrified the whole time. The seizures happen frequently, and they control my life. Living with Schizencephaly as an adult, I am able to help families understand what seizures feel like. For that I suppose I am grateful, but I hate seizures all the same.

Over the course of the last few years I have found other adults with Unilateral Schizencephaly (meaning the damage is located primarily on one side of the brain). Most of them have similar issues; partial paralysis, headaches, over all pain, and yes, even seizures.

I wanted to share my story so parents with nonverbal children can understand what living with Schizencephaly is like. Although I do not know why I was chosen for this journey, I have learned to live this way. Some days it feels like I am so overpowered by my Schizencephaly, and there is very little that I can do except wait. I never know when or where a seizure will happen, I only know that I will have one eventually.

For me, my family is my support. Without them, life would be even scarier. If there was more research and more people aware of Schizencephaly, things could be different. Science is just now tapping into innovative research, but we are nowhere near where we need to be yet. So I wait and live day-to-day with this overshadowing feeling that something always has a hold of my life that I cannot control.

TRICIA DENNIS and STEPHANIE ZIEMANN

Sadie

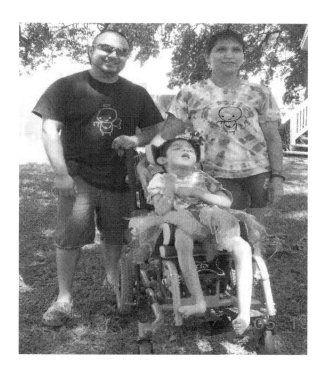

I was 16 and a senior in high school when I found out I was pregnant with Sadie. I didn't know I was pregnant until I was about three months along. Just like every other teen that finds out they are pregnant, I was scared to tell my parents, so I hid my pregnancy for another three months.

My first appointment with the doctor was to find what sex the baby was and if the baby was healthy. That appointment made a dramatic turn when the doctor told me he thought the baby might have a cyst on her brain, but he wanted me to go to The University of Texas Medical Branch (UTMB) in Galveston to get a second opinion. Gilbert (Sadie's father) and I talked about what the doctors told us already; if there was a cyst it was removable, or that it might not be anything. They never showed us the ultrasound that they did, so we didn't know exactly what they saw.

The day of the appointment at UTMB everything was going great. We went up there thinking everything was going to be ok. We had our worries, but we didn't let them get the best of us until we knew for sure what was going on. When the nurse came in to do the ultrasound, she was upbeat and showing us our little girl's fingers and toes. As the nurse was showing us our little girl's face and taking measurements, she got quiet. I looked over at the nurse, and she had tears coming down her face. All I could do was look at her and wonder what was going on. What did she see in that picture that we didn't? Then, all of a sudden, she excused herself and told us she would be right back with the doctor. While the nurse was gone I told my family that we had decided on a name for our baby, Sadie Nicole Perez.

A few minutes later the doctor came in to look at the ultrasound. He showed us a black area on the screen where Sadie's brain was and said it looked like there was a lot of fluid on the brain, and he would like to do an MRI to get a better look at her. Of course I started to freak out about the fluid on Sadie's brain and the effects it could have on her. Then I started to worry about the fact I had never heard of them doing an MRI on a pregnant woman. The doctor assured us it was safe to do and we had nothing to worry about. He should have thought those words through a little bit better. I had a lot to worry about.

The MRI appointment was set up for the same day. It took forever because Sadie was doing a lot of kicking. The doctors kept telling me not to move. I told them it wasn't me, it was Sadie; they needed to tell her to sit still. The doctors finally got what they needed and allowed me come in the room to see how it looked with Sadie in my tummy, which was neat. Of course they didn't show me anything else.

Hours later, the doctor finally came to tell us the results of what was found. He started off by asking me if I had been in any type of accident since I had gotten pregnant, and I told him no. That's when he told us our daughter had a rare brain disorder called Schizencephaly. Life as we knew it changed forever.

After hearing the words, "Your daughter has Schizencephaly," the doctor explained to us what he was able to find and gave us an internet printout to help explain the condition.

He said, "The cause of this is really unknown. That's why I was asked if any type of accident has happened that would have harmed the baby, to help pinpoint a reason for this happening." We are all crying at this point, and then he then told me, "There is a large chance that Sadie won't make it through the delivery, but it is too late in the pregnancy to abort."

It would not have made a difference if this had been discovered earlier, aborting was not an option. Sadie was ours from the time I found out, and there was no way I would have let that happen. If my grandmother could raise my uncle who had Cerebral Palsy all by herself, Gilbert and I could do this. And we would, no matter what.

It was late when we left the hospital, so we stayed at a hotel in Galveston. I remember laying in bed that night crying and holding my belly. I had blamed myself for not getting in to see a doctor sooner; that maybe this happened to Sadie because I didn't get the care I needed to from the beginning. The doctor told me that this wasn't my fault, even if I would have gotten into a doctor sooner there was nothing I could have done to prevent this. I think of it this way; I got to avoid the doctors trying to push me to abort by saying it's for the best. I told myself that by not going I never had to hear those horrible words.

We tried to learn all we could about Schizencephaly over the next few months. We had limited internet access, and there really wasn't much to find anyway, except the same information over and over.

I ended up going into early labor at one point and the doctors were able to stop it. They wanted Sadie to wait a little longer before making her entrance into the world. We ended up having to stay at a facility for high-risk pregnant women in Galveston.

I went into labor again two weeks later. The birth went really well and without any complications. Sadie came into the world on May 8, 2002. She weighed 5 pounds 3 ounces, with a head full of hair and lungs as strong as they could be. I got to see her for a brief moment before they rushed her out of the room to make sure everything was ok with her. When I finally got to see her, I knew she was going to be just fine. The doctors didn't give her a chance from the day they diagnosed her, but she proved them wrong. And it wouldn't be the last time.

The morning after Sadie was born; the nurses came in to get all the information about us for Sadie's birth certificate and other important papers. I remember sitting there and the nurse asked if we were giving Sadie up for adoption. I know it was probably a mandatory question, but I took it personally. First thing I thought was the nurse assumed that just because Sadie was going to have special needs that I would give her up. Then I thought she was thinking that because I was a young mother I would want to give her up. I snapped at the nurse, not thinking that maybe she was just doing her job. I just felt like she thought I wouldn't want my little girl. Guess that goes to show a mother's natural instinct to protect her child.

I was released from the hospital two days later, but Sadie had to stay. They wanted Sadie to gain a few more ounces before they let her go home. We ended up renting a hotel room so I could be there morning, noon, and night to feed her. Sadie gained the weight that they wanted her to, and she was allowed to come home. The day that she was released fell on Mother's Day. The trip back home was a little overwhelming with a newborn that was not comfortable in the car seat, but being able to finally take her home was the best gift I could have received.

Things were going well over the next few months. We went back to Galveston for several appointments with different specialists and had an MRI done to confirm that Sadie had Schiz. I remember looking at the images and wondering how on earth something like this could happen. The images were so disturbing to me at the time because I still didn't quite understand what Schizencephaly was.

We started to see the developmental delays the doctors had told us to watch for. Sadie wasn't holding her head up, rolling over, or grabbing for objects. I knew to expect this, but it still hurt not to be able to watch my daughter do these things. It was especially hard since we lived with my sister at the time, and she had her daughter who was a year older then Sadie. So you can imagine what I was going through.

I refused to admit that Sadie would never be able to do these things. The doctors had told me that the side of the brain that Sadie was missing the most of was the side that controlled the motor skills, but they also told me that it was possible for the other side of her brain to make up for it and learn for the side that was missing. I held on to that little bit of information.

Sadie did great over the next couple of years. We had therapists coming to the house to work with her. We had physical, occupational, vision, and speech therapies. It was decided that Sadie would start Pre-K a year early so she could get more use out of the therapy at school with the equipment they were introducing her to.

This was also the time she started having her first seizures. The doctors had told us that seizures could start at any time and to watch for them. The first couple of seizures were the worst. She would arch her back, her eyes would roll back, she would hold her breath, and become so stiff. We rushed Sadie to the hospital, hoping that they could do something, but by the time we would get there the seizure was over and she would do nothing but sleep. They told us to contact her doctor the next day. This just frustrated me, I wanted them to do something right then and there so the seizures would stop, but I found no help there.

I got her in to see her local doctor before we could go see her doctors in Galveston. Sadie's pediatrician had an EEG done, but they took too long and were unable to get anything from it. We went to Galveston to see her doctors and have them take care of the seizures. They decided to put Sadie on Phenobarbital. After the first dose we had to go right back to the emergency room because Sadie's body was red. It wasn't like a typical rash; she was just red, and it was spreading. She had had an allergic reaction to the medicine. The hospital was at least able to get a hold of the doctors in Galveston so they could change medications. They put Sadie on Topamax to control the seizures. As time went by we had to increase the dosage because little seizures started to slip through.

Sadie's arms started to get very tight, and she was also put on Baclofen for her muscle tone. Even now, we can't get her to stretch her arms all the way out because they are so tight.

Things were going well for a while. Sadie was in school and getting all the therapy that she needed through them. We finally accepted that Sadie's motor skills would never develop and that she would not be able to hold her head up or have any trunk support. We still tried anything that the doctors suggested in hopes that maybe she would still develop the ability to do these things.

Of course, just when everything seems to be going well, something always comes up. Once again we were in Galveston for a checkup with Sadie's team of doctors. They were doing the usual measuring, making sure the wheelchair is working out, and that her AFO's weren't giving her any trouble. Then they told us that Sadie's hip seems to be out of place, and that we needed to make an appointment with her orthopedic doctor. We made the appointment, and he told us that Sadie would need surgery and as soon as possible in order to fix her hip.

They performed the surgery in February, 2009. After she was out of the operating room and recovery, they moved her to a private room. This was the first time I really got to see Sadie's whole body. Well, not really her whole body, she was in a cast from her hips down to the knee, with only a big enough opening to be able to put her diaper on, and a cast on her ankle. Since they were already doing surgery, the orthopedic doctor decided to go ahead and try to fix

Sadie's right ankle which was turning in by trying stretch those tendons to see if it would help.

Seeing my little girl in pain and wrapped in those casts was hard. Even though I knew she had to have them so the surgery would not be in vain, I didn't like it one bit. Sadie was in the hospital for a week after her surgery. We had planned ahead and rented a small beach house for everyone to stay at, but I stayed with Sadie at nights, only leaving to shower and eat. You can imagine how happy we all were when they said she was ready to go home, which wasn't the easiest thing since she was in this cast that had her legs pushed out like a frog. It was a long trip home. Sadie had to lay down in the back seat, and I sat on protective guard next to her.

When we made it home, we moved Sadie's bed and everything she would possibly need into the living room and got her settled in. Unfortunately we couldn't stay settled in for long. The pharmacy that we had the hospital call the prescriptions into was closed. We had to have the hospital resend the prescriptions to a 24 hour pharmacy that was 45 minutes away. It seemed like we would never get there, and I knew the medicine that she had in her system was wearing off.

After we finally got everything situated, things started to run smoothly. Although baths, diaper changes, and getting at least a shirt on her wasn't the easiest. We started cutting the backs of the shirts open like the hospital gowns so she wouldn't have to be moved as much when putting them on.

After Sadie was cut out of the casts, and the doctors were

pleased with how well she was doing, she stayed out of school the rest of that year, there were only two months left anyway. From there she continued to improve. The ankle surgery didn't take like we had hoped it would, but that was one small thing compared to her hips.

For the past couple of years, Sadie has done really well. She went back to school the next year and continues her therapy there. She no longer receives vision or speech therapy because since there has been no signs of change in these areas, we all agreed that they would discontinue them for the time being. Sadie has also been enjoying Challenger Baseball, which is a league set up for all special needs children in the area. She loves being outside and around others, so this has been great.

Currently, we are in the process of getting Sadie a back brace to help reverse her Scoliosis. Over the years we have watched her back slowly curve, the doctors weren't too worried about it since she wasn't in any pain and it wasn't affecting her in any way. I have always thought something needed to be done, but every time I asked them about getting a brace in the past they told me it wasn't necessary. With Sadie's back looking worse, I started to worry more. I finally got the courage to let the doctors know that I thought it would help her more if she had one. I wouldn't have been able to do this without all the outstanding support of the other Schiz moms. With all the encouragement I received from them and their opinions on the subject, I found my voice on the matter with the doctor.

Last year, Sadie participated in the first Schizencephaly Day of

Awareness, and so many people came out to support her.

Her journey is one that touches so many when she meets them, and I feel blessed I was chosen to be her mom. Things can get hard at times without having all the answers about Schiz that we would like, but I wouldn't change a thing. Sadie is perfect the way she is. She has taught me so much about life that I didn't know. It's amazing how far she has come, and I know that as days go by, she will go even further.

TRICIA DENNIS and STEPHANIE ZIEMANN

Jaylen

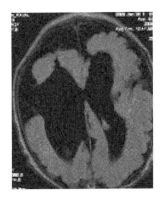

"Your daughter is going to be mentally retarded."

That was the last statement I thought I'd ever hear as I was holding my precious baby girl that was only a few hours old. Those words struck hard, causing instantaneous crying. The doctor, who was obviously lacking bedside manner, not to mention being absent of morals and sensitivity, proceeded to explain that my daughter, Jaylen, had developed Hydrocephalus and would be severely delayed in life. I was stunned as a first time mother who had four ultrasounds during my pregnancy, and none had given any hint as to what was happening within my daughter's brain. She looked perfectly healthy! In my denial of her diagnosis, I was able to stop crying and look that doctor in the eye and ask for a second opinion. A few hours later, another doctor came in and notified me that Jaylen would have to be airlifted to a specialty hospital in Gainesville, Florida to get an MRI done.

Walking into the NICU at Shands Hospital was a surreal experience. I remember feeling it was an out-of-body experience because I felt so disconnected from reality. The nurse led me to Jaylen, laying peacefully in slumber, like nothing was wrong. All I could do was stand there and cry. Everything I had planned, dreamed, and hoped for had all just crashed down in a few hours time.

After my tears had calmed, I started to look around Jaylen's area and noticed a binder with my daughter's name and a word I'd never seen or heard of before written below it. It read "Schizencephaly". Little did I know that that single stretch of letters would forever change our lives. No doctors had come to see us yet, so I Googled the word on my phone and began to read what very little information is available on the diagnosis.

Nine days later, I was able to leave Shands with Jaylen. Somber is the only word to describe that moment of my life. Looking back on it now, I realize that I don't remember much from early on in her life. It's all a haze of appointments, CT scans, lab work, and X-ray's that are all strung together in one big mess of depression. Jaylen was as healthy as I could ask for, besides the colds that would always require a doctor's visit and chest X-ray's. Whenever I would try to explain to someone what condition she had, it was always the same response, "What's that?" Followed by "Is it curable?" And I would have to tell them sadly, no.

As Jaylen started to get older, things became more noticeable. Like how she never learned the suck-swallow-breathe coordination, which was crucial to her being able to eat on her own. She never attempted to crawl and would scream if you would put her on her belly. She wasn't receiving adequate nutrition on her own, so I decided to move forward with the placement of a feeding tube. That further prevented her from receiving the tummy time she desperately needed. Watching other mothers with their "normal" children was painful. I remained hopeful, but have always been a bit of a pessimist. I can now admit I was sour about it, but that soon changed.

I can distinctly remember the exact reason why my perspective on both Jaylen's and my lives changed. I was at Jaylen's pediatrician's office and this mother sitting across from me was moving around a lot which caught my attention. When I looked up and noticed that she was pushing her kids out of their seats and across the room and made the comment to her children, "I don't want you near people like that." I was livid and seeing red. That was the first time someone had actually ever made a comment that I could actually hear about my daughter. Sure, I'd heard the whispers and seen the stares, but I brushed them all off. Ignorance is common. From that point on, I had quit looking at Jaylen and me as victims. I have since taken a very strong stance on awareness and anti-bullying in all aspects.

In these past four years, Jaylen has taught me so much more than anyone else ever could. She has taught me patience, which helps greatly with all the doctor's appointments and hospital stays. She has taught me to pay attention to details, what may be a simple cold or congestion can turn into full blown pneumonia if you're not attentive. She's also taught me simple and pure admiration. She doesn't know she's not like other children, I don't think she would care even if she did. Through all her tough times and close calls with death knocking on the door, she's been a fighter. She has such a bright and happy personality, and she's smiling constantly. Thanks to the never ending support of family and friends, our journey has been much easier.

I was told that Jaylen wouldn't make it past six months. Oh, how little faith doctors have! Jaylen has been proving them wrong for three and a half years now, and we're looking forward to many more.

TRICIA DENNIS and STEPHANIE ZIEMANN

Valentina

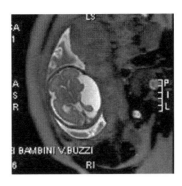

I was 20 years old when I was pregnant with my daughter, and I wasn't ready for a baby. And it didn't help that my mum had just kicked me and my siblings out of our apartment.

One day, my mum said she was going to visit a friend and she didn't want to see us the next morning. She then checked if we were packing our things. My sister and I packed everything we could, and my brother went to work. We put our stuff in my boyfriend's garage and waited. We had nowhere to go. Luckily we searched an apartment days before and received a callback later that day to look at an apartment for rent.

I was pregnant at that time. My period was always irregular, so I didn't worry. I had my period like always, but one day it was strange. I Googled it and found that it was a sign of pregnancy. I took a test and it was positive. I immediately went to our hospital and got an ultrasound. The doctor said, "Congratulations! You will have a daughter and you are at the beginning of the fourth month. "I was shocked. I couldn't believe it.

I went home and calculated and thought about it. Then I cried because I didn't know what to do. What kind of woman doesn't know she's pregnant? I felt as though I didn't deserve this baby. I thought there was something wrong and it was my fault because I didn't pay attention. I didn't realize it. Plus, I didn't know how to raise a child, and had no one to ask for advice. The only example I had was my mother, and she was abusive. She beat us, criticized us constantly, called us names, and gave us horrible punishments like kneeling in rice for hours. We didn't have a kitchen or hot water, and there was garbage everywhere in the apartment. What kind of mother would I be?

Where I live, you have to make appointments at the hospital yourself. When I went to make an appointment, the hospital said the earliest I could see a doctor was in two months. I was perplexed. I told them I was in the fourth month and have never been checked. The nurse looked suspicious and asked me if I was sure the doctor had said month and not week.

I knew something wasn't right, so my boyfriend and I went to another hospital. I lied and said that my stomach hurt and that I never had a checkup. The doctor was very nice and told us that everything was ok. I was two weeks further along than what the previous doctor had said, and that we need to go see our doctor. I was still not sure. I told my boyfriend there is something wrong. Why did I have my period if I was pregnant?

Two months later we went to the appointment that was made at the first hospital. The doctor said something was wrong with the baby's brain. He made an appointment for us with the head of department, and he said he suspected it was Schizencephaly. There was some kind of fluid on her brain, but he couldn't tell if it was blood, water, or something else. This doctor said he couldn't confirm it and that we should go to a specialist at another hospital. My heart felt like it had fallen onto the ground. I was beside myself trying to understand what I was hearing.

The hospital wasn't big; we live in a small town with less than 40,000 people, so we were sent to the hospital in the main city of the province. It was probably for the best. The doctors in our town are really nice, but I got the feeling that they were not sure how to deal with our situation.

I wanted to know more, so, like always, I Googled it, but that didn't helped me much. I found the Wikipedia page and that was about it. I also found some books where it was mentioned, but they were all in English, and I didn't understand them. I read that people with Schizencephaly usually had Epilepsy, paralysis, hemispheres, mental retardation, and seizures. This all scared me. I didn't know what to do or how I could help my daughter.

Later on, we met the head of department at The Neonatal Intensive Care Station. He was very nice and told us that everything above could be, but could also not happen. He also mentioned that there is a possibility to go to Germany and have a late-term abortion in case of disability of the unborn child. We had already decided to keep the baby. He then told us we needed to do an MRI to be sure, and we were sent to the hospital in Milan.

It was then that I told my sister about the pregnancy. I had waited because I wasn't sure what to say to people, there was only the suspicion of Schizencephaly. I wanted to wait until I knew what happened, or until I had more information.

The four hour drive to Milan was tiring, but were hopeful. I was so happy and nervous and excited because finally I would know what to do. I would know what my baby has and how to help her.

It was scary in the MRI tube. The doctor said "Inhale. Hold your breath. Exhale." Then I heard someone say something, and the doctors laughed. I was ashamed and scared, and here they were laughing. I kept quiet and did what the doctors said because they were the specialist, and because I had come so far for information.

After the MRI, we waited for the results. I think my heart skipped a beat when the doctor said she was ready to talk to us. She confirmed the Schizencephaly. She told us there was a cyst near a cleft, and the Schizencephaly was probably bilateral. There was also something on the right side which they couldn't see clearly, and my daughter's head was really big, and still growing. I would have to have a caesarean operation because of her head being so big.

When I questioned why this happened, she said "Something happened during the pregnancy." These were the words I was waiting for? Needless to say, we went home disappointed. It was obvious to us that the doctors did not have much information on what Schizencephaly was at all.

My daughter was born November5, and we named her Valentina. She weighed 10 pounds, and scored 9.9 on the APGAR test. The doctors took her immediately to intensive care. They said she needed an operation because of the cyst. I went home after six days, but Valentina had to stay. It's a horrible feeling, going home without your baby. That's not how it's supposed to be.

Valentina is such a beautiful baby. She has a strong mind and is a fighter. The doctors had a neurological meeting and decided not to operate because Valentina was in much better condition as expected.

After 10 days, Valentina was finally able to go home, and the journey began. There were routine examinations, EEG's, physiotherapy, ergo-therapy, eye examinations, X-ray examinations, constant video monitoring.

The doctors would give us random appointments for the EEG's. Sometimes we had to wake her up at 4 or 5 in the morning (after she went to bed at midnight), and keep her awake until we had the appointment. They would put multiple electrodes on her head that shouldn't be moved. Then she was expected to fall asleep in a hospital room with new people and scared parents.

Also we recorded Valentina every night to see if she was having seizures in her sleep. Every move she made scared us because we didn't like what a seizure looked like. YouTube videos helped a lot to understand what a seizure looks like.

We did an ultrasound of Valentina's head when she was one month old. The nurse who was operating the machine told me she knew a mum whose son also had Schizencephaly, only not as severe as Valentina. She told me Valentina would not learn to walk before she the age of three. I was angry at the woman and became defensive. I didn't say anything out loud, but in my head I was thinking "She doesn't know me. She doesn't know my life or my child. Valentina is not her friend's son." No one can predict what the brain is capable of!

Primarily I was sad that Valentina would not go to kindergarten, she wouldn't go with me to the park and play like other kids.

At the time it seemed to me that everybody had an opinion, but nobody had a cure or security. I know that every child has their own development, but what's the purpose of scaring the parents? Nobody explained what to do in case of a seizure, or in case one of the things they told us could happen did happen. They said Valentina could be physically and mentally disabled, she could be paralyzed one half of her body, she has a huge head, she could have seizures, she could be nourished through a tube. But what should we do if that happens? That left us scared and unprepared.

I recall the day when I was washing dishes and something felt wrong. Valentina was playing, but it was too quiet. I looked over and she was laying on the floor twitching. I didn't know what to do. I grabbed Valentina and ran to the neighbor's door. She called 911 and the paramedics came. I remembered to tell the paramedics about the videos of her sleeping and the twitching in her limbs.

I thought Epilepsy had begun. My world was crushed, and all I could do was cry. I had to return to my job, but I couldn't do anything and cried constantly. My boss let me go home, and I was dismissed after two weeks.

Luckily they were febrile seizures. Febrile seizures are brought on by high temperature spikes, and the doctor gave us Diazepam

(Valium) in case a seizure happened and told us what to do.

The most pleasant parts are the physical and ergo therapy. We have amazing therapists, and Valentina loves them.

I have to say that in the end, we were lucky. We have a beautiful and happy child. None of what the doctors predicted happened. When Valentina wants something, she will fight for it. The first time she was standing on her feet was a real milestone. I was thrilled. And then she began to walk, step by step. At first she fell so many times I thought she wasn't ready, but she never quit. Valentina learned to walk at 13 months, and all on her own merit. She does that with everything new. She repeats it over and over again until she can do it. I'm so proud of her.

We need research. The thing I hate the most about Schizencephaly is the not knowing. One day my daughter will grow up, and she deserves to know more about it. I want something more to tell her other than "something happened." Other parents need to know what will happen and what they should do. I have been so blessed to find others and people fighting for awareness for this disorder. If not for my own peace of mind but for the people just learning of this disorder and the possibilities it could be prevented. I am grateful to be able to share my story and I hope in this small glimpse of my life someone will become more aware of this disorder.

Makenley

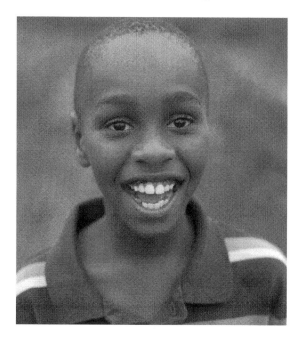

We first met Makenley in December of 2003, when he was 16 months old. We had been in the process of his adoption from Haiti for several months, but this was our first trip there. It was a meeting that was everything we had hoped for when embarking on the journey of parenthood for the first time. He took to his mother right away, and a permanent bond was formed. There was nothing indicating any issues medically because he was still very young, so we felt extremely blessed to have found such a wonderful young boy in such bleak circumstances.

It wasn't until a couple months later, when Jackie visited with her mother, that we began to notice something may be a little off. Makenley had been very sick prior to mom's arrival, and was not allowed to leave the orphanage for the first few days of the visit due to the fact that he was receiving his fluids and nutrients intravenously because of aspiration caused by his then unknown condition.

We began to piece together other signs as well, such as Makenley being relatively non-verbal and not being able to walk on his own. There was nothing substantial medically to give us any clue as to what may be transpiring with Makenley beyond the belief that he may have had a stroke at some point during his maturation, which caused his right side to be weak, and other factors such as drooling and a decreased gag reflex.

With the aid of our U.S. Senator, we were able to get Makenley home five months later. At 23 months, which ultimately proved to be another significant milestone, Makenley's health was on a bit of a decline. We were fortunate to get matched up with the International Adoption Center and its team of doctors at Riley Hospital in Indianapolis, in conjunction with our initial neurological evaluation. It was this evaluation that changed Makenley's prognosis and the course of our lives.

I remember the visit to the doctor for the results of his MRI and thinking, "It's cool. We'll get him some therapy, work with him to build his strength and esteem, and everything will be great." Boy, was I off on that prediction.

We were sitting in a couple of chairs in the consultation room when the doctor came in and threw the charts up on the viewing monitor. I remember doing a double take because I couldn't quite grasp what I was seeing. The left frontal lobe of Makenley's brain was void of any formation.

The doctor began by saying, "Your son has a rare condition called Open Lip Schizencephaly. It is a condition which occurs in-utero, and is most recognizable by the malformation of the brain. Most people can relate to the condition medically if we refer to its more commonplace name, Cerebral Palsy."

I remember sitting there stunned. I thought we would walk in, get a script for some therapy, be told he needed to do some muscle building exercises, and be on our way. I kept looking from Makenley innocently playing over by the door, to the monitor, at the doctor, then back to Makenley. I kept thinking "How can this be? He seems so... normal."

Then I asked a question that would become the defining moment of Makenley's life here with us and, ultimately, his development. "What does this mean for him long-term? I mean, I'm looking at him now and he appears to be a regular two year old kid."

"This might be all you'll ever get out of him," was the neurologist's response.

I sat there looking at this man in a stunned silence, thrown back by the cold, clinical nature of his response. I told him, "Well, that just isn't good enough." And with that we collected our things, including the diagnostic findings and images, and went to Riley, Ohio. We never saw that neurologist again.

We immediately got Makenley enrolled in a program where he could receive speech, physical, and occupational therapies. He seemed to adjust well to the therapists, and really enjoyed going to his sessions and learning new things. Riley had begun a medication to assist with his drooling. He also began receiving routine Botox injections in his feet, calves, and hands, in an effort to relieve some of the tension brought on by the tightening of his muscles and tendons; which continued to worsen as he aged.

We enrolled Makenley in a general education preschool at the age of three, where he remained for three more years until he went off to kindergarten at the age of six. Makenley thrived in the general class setting, and was challenged by one of the most affectionate and caring teachers we've ever met. She is directly responsible for the academic success and development he has enjoyed. She gave us the simple recommendation that Makenley should be challenged in a normal learning environment, where she truly believed he could thrive and mature. Obviously she recognized something we were too naïve to see and, with the assistance of an IEP, he has enjoyed immeasurable successes and been open to wonderful opportunities that otherwise may not have presented themselves.

The resilience Makenley has shown in every facet of his growth and maturity is astounding. Every time we doubt he can cross the next hurdle, he proves us wrong. We worry about situations that he may be confronted with academically or socially, but he deals with them, adapts, and overcomes. I'm convinced now that the best thing we can do for this bright, energetic child is to stay out of his way. We owe it to him to give him all the love and support that two parents can give, and stop impeding his progress because he is determined and will find a way.

If you didn't know Makenley and saw him in a social setting, you might think he's a normal 10 year old boy. He enjoys all of the things boys enjoy, like video games, basketball, and soccer. He also likes being with his friends, going to parties, and riding his bike. Yes, riding his bike.

It's not until you get to know him a little bit more that you recognize the physical traits which he possesses that aren't quite like yours and mine. Makenley does drool on occasion. It occurs mostly when he is highly stimulated or concentrating on a certain subject. We have been able to curtail a lot of this through medication and awareness as he's gotten older, but it does still exist. He walks with a slight limp, and has obvious right-sided weakness. This means most of the damage from the in–utero stroke was caused to the left side of the brain. The effects of these physical challenges have been addressed through surgery to lengthen the tendons in his right foot and heel to reduce the stress on his leg which caused him to walk on his tip toes; and muscle and flexibility exercises given to him by his PT.

In my opinion, the two things that stand out the most about Makenley are his impulsiveness in certain situations, and his slurred speech. Makenley has had to go through extensive behavioral therapies and evaluations because the portion of the brain which control these attitudes, or tendencies, is not present with Makenley. We have addressed the speech issue by continuing his therapy through school and outside sources. He is currently enrolled in an intense program offered through Butler University, where they challenge Makenley with his speech clarity and enunciation. This is probably the primary area of concern for us as parents because as his peers move forward and continue to develop, we fear he may become alienated due to the obvious nature of his differences. Of course, as he has done in every other incident, I'm sure he will prove us wrong again.

We feel very fortunate that the degree of Makenley's affectedness from Schizencephaly is fairly mild when compared to some cases we've seen and read about. He receives A's and B's on his report cards, plays team sports, is highly adaptable in most settings, loves and hates his siblings, and lives a fairly normal life by comparison. It's lent itself to some guilt on my part when I compare his situation to that of some others, but then I realize we're not out of the woods yet. He still is prone to seizures (which he has not experienced yet), and we don't know the ultimate degree of his long-term independence.

One thing we know for certain is that we are blessed to be his parents, and the people that truly get to know Makenley are blessed by their experience as well. By God's grace, Makenley was spared a dire fate in his homeland and has something special to give back to this world. And it's our duty to help him overcome this disorder and develop that gift, wherever that may lead him in this life.

TRICIA DENNIS and STEPHANIE ZIEMANN

Rey

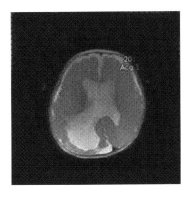

My fiancé and I found out I was pregnant in January 2011. After having two previous miscarriages, I was very nervous and believed I could not have children. I went to my gynecologist and it was discovered that I was insulin resistant and found out it could have something to do with my not being able to become pregnant. They put me on a drug called Metformin, and I was pregnant within two months.

I was very sick throughout my entire pregnancy and had to be on bed rest at 19 weeks because I would bleed from overexerting myself. I was not doing too much in my eyes, but I guess my body could not handle the pregnancy and my normal routine. Rey was a very active baby, and seemed to be developing right. I enjoyed being pregnant, even as hard as it was.

When I was 28 weeks pregnant, I had another incident where I was bleeding and needed to go to the emergency room. They thought I was miscarrying, but I was not. They wanted to do a routine ultrasound to make sure Rey was doing well and that my placenta was in the right place.

It seemed like hours went by after the ultrasound, and we

wondered why they were keeping me for so long. A group of doctors walked in and said they needed to have a serious conversation with us. I was panicking because of my other miscarriages, and confused because I just saw him moving on the ultrasound screen and heard his heartbeat. They started by telling us that Rey was fine, but they discovered something that needed to be addressed on his brain. We kept asking them questions and it seemed like every answer was "We don't know yet, you need to speak with a specialist." They referred us to perinatal doctor and sent us on our way with no answers.

First we met with the specialist at the high-risk pregnancy center two weeks later. He went over our ultrasound and told us he believed Rey had Hydrocephalus. He wanted to do twice-weekly non-stress tests, his own extensive ultrasound, and try to get me in for an MRI to check Rey's head size. He also told us of the possibility of Rey having a shunt implanted shortly after birth if the fluid on his brain was over excessive to take the access fluid and drain it into his abdominal cavity. Next we met with a neurosurgeon for a consultation and the RNICU. We were told when Rey was born we would have a team of doctors and nurses from the RNICU in the room. I also was told I might not be able to have a vaginal birth if Rey's head size was too large.

I had to get an ultrasound every 2-3 weeks. I didn't get to have an MRI because the office couldn't fit me into their schedule, and the prenatal doctor was unable figure out why Rey's head was so large without one. He looked at the ventricles on Rey's brain and said they were working just fine, but there were various black spots on Rey's brain. This doctor also had no answers or diagnosis for us. He still believed it may be Hydrocephalus, but then would question himself.

I was sent to have an ultrasound 39 weeks because of terrible back pain, and it felt like Rey was not acting right. The ultrasound showed that my water had broken and I was leaking my fluid very slowly. They decided to induce me, which became a two day process. I was having contractions, but I wasn't dilating. Rey's oxygen level remained steady even through the contractions, so they put me on oxygen to help. I ended up falling asleep and was awoken at two in the morning for an emergency C-section because Rey's oxygen level dropped. No sooner then they told me, I was in a room being prepped for surgery.

On August 19, 2011, at 2:36 A.M., my baby boy, Reymundo, was born. He was having trouble breathing so they took him away and would not let me see him. It broke my heart not being able to hold him for his first moments of life. My fiancé followed them up to the RNICU and took pictures to show me when they stabilized Rey. My fiancé told me later it took a while for them to stabilize him and to get him to breathe.

I was able to go see Rey later that day. When I saw him, I absolutely fell in love. He was in an incubator with an IV in his foot, and on oxygen. When they let me hold my boy for the first time, I was so weak. I only held him for a few moments and I had to give him back to the nurse. When we were about to leave the room for the night, the nurses told me all the tests they were going to do on

Rey, and what we could expect for the days to come. If I was not sleeping or waiting on meds, I was up on that floor with my baby boy doing everything I could to find out what was going on.

The day after Rey was born; a neonatologist came to my room to discuss what they knew about Rey. She told us the perinatal doctor had diagnosed Rey wrong, he did not have Hydrocephalus, but she did not know what was wrong with him and needed to do more research. She wanted to meet with us in her office the next day.

We were in that neonatologist's office bright and early. I was so completely and utterly terrified; I could feel myself shaking with fear for my sweet little boy. Then we found out what Rey's diagnosis was. It was a brain disorder called Schizencephaly; it was like having holes or mountains on your brain. We were told Rey had Bilateral Type 2 Schizencephaly, which is one of the worst kinds. She showed us an MRI of Rey's brain and where his clefts (holes) were located. She had never seen this before in her hospital and had to refer to the medical books on her shelves to find out what it was. She also told us that Rey was going to have a hard life. He may never walk, talk, see, or hear because of where the clefts were in his brain. Then she made various appointments with doctors, therapists and social workers to come in and speak with us.

Over the next few days we met with a genealogist, a neurologist, a physical therapist, a neurosurgeon, a social worker, and an optometrist. The genealogist appointment was probably the hardest appointment for us, but he did have more information about

Schizencephaly than anyone else had. He told us Rey was going to be more prone to seizures, Hydrocephalus, and Cerebral Palsy. Rey could also be mentally retarded, and may never be able to be like a normal little boy. But he also said there was a chance that Rey could be completely normal, with only a few things wrong that would not be noticeable. He told us it was up to little Rey's brain trying to rewire itself and how bad the damage already was. We completely broke down. I could not understand how my little boy's life could be so hard after only a few days in this world. With tears rolling down his face, the neurologist told us not to lose hope. We asked if this was genetic, he said it was proven not to be in some cases, and in others it was. In Rey's case it was not genetic, but they did not know the cause of his Schizencephaly. He said something happened during Rey's 5-8 weeks gestation that caused his brain to not develop properly, causing the Schizencephaly, but we may never know what. It could have been anything from me being sick, to Rey having an in-utero stroke.

The next appointment was with a neurologist. He met with us and told us the same things. He laughed at us and asked why were we worrying now? If I had not have had such a rough pregnancy, no one would have known this baby was any different. He said yes, Rey could not breathe at birth, but no one would have known to give him an MRI if I had not had an ultrasound when I was pregnant. That made us feel a little better, but we were still devastated. The other appointments went just the same; them telling us they could not notice anything wrong at this time, and we would just have to wait and see.

Rey ended up being discharged from the RNICU seven days after his birth. We were sent home with a packet of referrals and information on what to do next. We decided as a family that I needed to stay home with Rey and take care of him. I was in the National Guard and going to college until I was put on bed rest.

I planned on going back to school again and getting a job after Rey was born, but that was put on hold. I was also supposed to be deploying in a year, and I knew I would not be able to leave him here with all the care he needed. Everything was on hold to make sure I could be there for him as much as possible. It was the best decision I have ever made.

We met with numerous doctors and physical therapists over the next eight weeks. Not one of the doctors we seen knew what Schizencephaly was, and actually admitted they had never seen it before. We were dumbfounded on the lack of research or knowledge about Schizencephaly. Rey was enrolled in a program with physical therapy and nurses that came to our house to check on him, and was also enrolled in physical therapy at the hospital. We had an optometrist appointment and they told us Rey was not blind. This was very reassuring because of where Rey's clefts were located in his brain. The physical therapists saw him once a week and did not notice any abnormalities, at first.

Rey had multiple MRI's and EEG's. The MRI showed Rey had the beginnings of Hydrocephalus and Microcephaly. The Hydrocephalus was not bad enough to give Rey a shunt and we would just have to monitor him. His EEG's did show abnormal brain waves, and that he was most likely going to have seizures. He had weekly appointments checking on his head size with therapy and the specialists, and was very well monitored. When we asked each doctor or specialist anything about Rey's condition or outcome, they always said we would have to wait and see.

It was six months later, and Rey was still doing really well. He was progressing, and neither side of his body was not showing any weaknesses, which the therapists loved. He had one seizure, but was not showing any more activity, so the neurologist did not recommend any meds. He was also rolling over and smiling. Rey was a very happy baby, and we never saw him as anything different.

At eight months, Rey's physical therapist noticed his hands shook a little when Rey was holding something or trying to put his hands to his mouth. It took Rey longer to learn things other babies were doing, and he was a little behind in his milestones. The therapist noticed the hands shaking more and more, and said he had tremors. We began noticing the tremors in his hands, legs, and even torso as time went on. He also was only army crawling and was too weak to crawl on hands and knees. The physical therapist mentioned that Rey was a little low toned, but he had hopes of crawling on all fours.

With every little milestone, my fiancé and I were jumping for joy. Every new thing Rey was doing was proving to those doctors that our Rey could beat his diagnosis. He was doing more than we ever believed he would be able to do.

Rey had another seizure when he was nine months old. His dad was vacuuming, and I went into Rey's room to hold him because he had been napping in his crib, and I did not want the vacuum frighten him. Rey woke up, so I laid him on the floor to change his diaper. When his dad began running the vacuum, Rey peed on me and started having bad tremors on the floor with a blank stare. I ran and yelled for his dad to turn off the vacuum and come in the room. Rey shook in my arms for 45 seconds. After he came out of his stare, he continued to tremor a lot and sweat, then he went back to sleep while still having the tremors. It was one of the scariest moments of my life. I know some kids have seizures daily, but seeing my own kid have one was heart breaking. The moms who see their kids have seizures daily are probably the strongest moms out there.

After the seizure, we called to schedule another appointment with the neurologist. He never even called us back. We had to call numerous times just to get him on the phone. We finally got in to see the neurologist, and he gave us no answers. He blew us off and wrote a script for seizure medication. We did not like how the doctor was treating us, so we held onto prescription and never filled it because we wanted a second opinion first.

We decided to take Rey to the Motts Children's Hospital to see a different neurologist and to try to get more answers. That appointment showed true to our feelings. We found a great neurologist, and she gave us a rescue seizure medication for Rey. She did not want to put him on daily meds because he was not having daily seizures. She said the tremors were not affecting his daily life, and she did not want to medicate him because it could delay him more than he already was. We agreed with her and were happy someone was finally answering our questions.

Rey has had one other seizure when he was 16 months old. Rey was sleeping in bed with us one night. After a few hours, he started crying out in his sleep, his legs and arms were shaking badly, and he was breathing heavily. It lasted about a minute, and he went right back to sleep. It seems like the seizures are few and far between, but they are scary none the less.

Rey's older sister has also made a huge impact Rey's development. At first we never told her anything about what was wrong with Rey, just that Rey needed a little more help than the other kids needed. She was five, so she took that answer without question. When she started getting older she wanted to know why people came to see Rey, and why he had so many appointments. We made a decision then to tell her what Schizencephaly was. We told her the word and described it as Rey having special needs because parts of his brain are missing. We told her that Rey needed to learn differently, and we needed to help him as much as possible. She took it very well and started kissing him ten times as much as before. She wanted to start participating in therapy and asking what we needed to do to help him. She also took him for show and tell. She told her class how her brother was born with holes in his brain. Rey could do the Itsy Bitsy Spider, crawl around faster than any baby she had ever seen, and she was more proud of him than anything else. She also said she admired him for everything he does. She ended up making her teacher and I cry. Rey's diagnosis definitely brought our family closer together in our fight to help Rey's progress.

When Rey turned a year old, we slowed down his physical therapy. He was going once a week to the hospital for therapy, and a therapist came to our home once a week. He was beginning to have anxiety about public and not performing at the hospital, and we decided to just have therapy in the home. Rey's physical in-home therapist is amazing. We could not ask for a better therapist. She recommended a front walker for Rey, and he is cruising around everywhere with it. Rey can take about 5-10 steps if he is not having tremors. He has a walker he uses, and cruises all over the place. He can stand for a little while, but sometimes is unstable. His speech is delayed, but he can say about 12 words. He has physical therapy once a week and occupational therapy every other week. He also wears glasses because he has bad vision and a weak eye. If the glasses do not help soon, he may have surgery. The neurosurgeon keeps an eye on the fluid on his brain (Hydrocephalus) with MRI's. The neurologist monitors Rey every six months now, and he has had multiple EEG's. Overall, he is doing amazingly for what we were told in the beginning.

Rey is now 19 months old, and he is an amazing little guy. I personally think he is doing great. Rey smiles at almost every stranger he meets, but he will not go near them. He is a definite Mama's boy and Daddy's boy. He loves to sing songs like Itsy Bitsy Spider, Twinkle Twinkle Little Star, and Patty Cake. His other favorite thing to do is read books with me. I read 10 books a day for him, sometimes more. With every little milestone, my fiancé and I are jumping for joy. Every new thing Rey does proves to those doctors that our Rey can beat his diagnosis. He is doing more than we ever believed he would.

Schizencephaly has definitely changed our lives, but I would not change anything for the world. We are scared about what the future holds for Rey, and yet we know everything will be all right as long as we love him and are there for him as much as possible. Things could have been a lot worse for Rey in the beginning, and many other kids have it worse off, so we feel truly blessed with how much our son has done so far.

To this day, the doctors still don't know what Rey's outcome will be. We pray to God for some kind of awareness.

TRICIA DENNIS and STEPHANIE ZIEMANN

Faith

I had my last ultrasound for my baby girl on June 7, 2002, and was due in six days. The ultrasound technician looked at the baby and quickly walked out. Then the doctor came in, looked at the ultrasound and said, "You need to get over to the Elmendorf Hospital as soon as possible. They just want to check on the baby's heart rate." The doctor refused to give us any more information, claiming that he would be held liable if he did.

Rick and I left the hospital and went over to the base hospital where I we found out that the baby's head was too small, and they wanted her to be born right away. In the time it took us to get some food and the clothes from the house, all kinds of things were flowing through my mind; but nothing like what was about to happen 24 hours from that moment.

We went back to the hospital later that afternoon and were admitted to labor and delivery. They tried all kinds of things to induce my labor that night, but nothing worked. I was started on Pitocin at 6:30 the following morning and labor moved much faster. I knew something wasn't right the moment the doctor tried to break my water because nothing came out. I ended up having a dry birth. I'm not shocked when I think about it now because I was in L&D about 3-5 days a week for the last trimester. I complained that something just wasn't right and it felt like the baby had dropped. All they did was hook me up to fetal and contraction monitors, and when nothing happened, they sent me home. I am certain this is the main reason the other hospital said I needed to be induced ASAP.

At 3:11 P.M. on June 8, our family went from two, to three. I didn't have a hard labor, really. Just a few pushes and Faith Anne was born. Her Apgar was a 9, hearing was the only thing she didn't pass. All in all she was a healthy baby girl. Little did we know that in the coming months we were going to find out a whole different story.

Rick received orders to serve at the Little Rock Air Force Base when Faith was four months old. At her first visit to the pediatric clinic the doctor told us we needed to see neurologist, ASAP.

We couldn't see the neurologist until months later. My mom came down to help us with that visit. They wanted to schedule an MRI six weeks down the road, but I said my mom was leaving in six days, so Faith's MRI was pushed to the following day. The results were read and it showed that Faith had clefts on her brain. We were told that she had Bilateral Schizencephaly. As brand new parents, what were we to do? It is one of those surreal moments where you hear someone talking but all you hear is an echo. The more he said, the less I began hearing as my mind drifted into panic.

Once that news kicked in, it was nothing but a downhill spiral.

We had horrible doctors. The pediatrician dropped Faith's case. Then Faith was not drinking and we decided to have a g-tube paced. The surgeon made her feeding tube incision too big and it leaked formula and food all the time, causing Faith to not gain weight. Because of the poor surgery, we were watching her slip away from us for four years. Was this the life she would live and was this our new normal?

Faith did attend a wonderful therapy clinic at the base, but unfortunately they discontinued her services because they didn't understand what to do for someone with her disorder. I wondered if this was the life she would live, and was this to be our new normal?

On August 21, 2007, Faith started throwing up and having diarrhea every day during her feedings. We would put her in her positioning chair, hook her up for a feed, and have to keep a tub near her face so she could vomit into it. After a few weeks, she was admitted to the hospital. They had no answers and sent her home. It went on like that for a few more weeks before Faith was admitted into the hospital again. After 11 days, as we were being discharged, a nurse said, "She's going to die anyway, she should go at home." Bedside manner is something I have learned to appreciate in this journey.

Faith was sick for six straight months and no one was willing to help her. We decided enough was enough and wanted to move back to Alaska. The Air Force was dead set on keeping Rick in Little Rock, even though it was a horrible place for Faith's health, but Rick contacted Alaska's Air National Guard about job openings. There were six different job openings. He applied for all of them, and got them all, but chose the one that would keep him closer to home.

Part of the reason we moved back to Alaska was to be near family, but mostly for better doctors. Faith's medical care here has been astounding. When we moved back in March of 2008, Faith weighed 18 pounds, she now weighs 45. That never would have happened in Arkansas.

We go through so many difficult times as special needs parents, especially with a disorder no one understands. There is nothing more amazing than knowing a child with special needs, they teach you how to appreciate the things we all stop paying attention to as a child; like the shape of clouds, or the sound of birds. We should all be as lucky as Faith, she sees the world the way it was meant to be seen; with love and an open heart.

Although we still do not fully understand Schizencephaly, I know we were given this road to travel for a reason. At the darkest moments, even when I thought I was losing her, I always had my Faith. And she knows I will continue fighting as long as I have breath in my body.

TRICIA DENNIS and STEPHANIE ZIEMANN

Baye

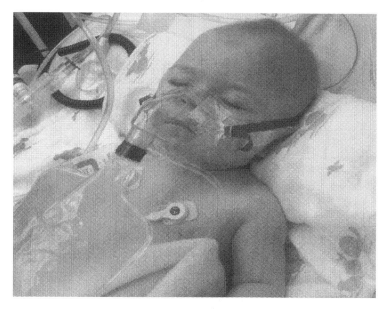

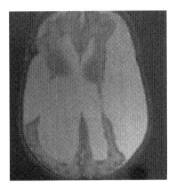

I was so nervous looking at those two pink lines after suffering two miscarriages. I had taken five tests to confirm that it was really positive. I really was pregnant! I called my doctor and made my first appointment.

My pregnancy was a breeze, I was never sick and I could eat anything I wanted. It was perfect. I always told people Baye was going to be a little devil because she never gave me any trouble. That was true, up until I was 26 weeks pregnant.

I went to the doctor one day because my chest felt heavy and I thought I was getting a cold. It wasn't a cold, I had developed preeclampsia and had fluid building up around my heart and lungs, making it unable for me to breathe and my heart slow down. The preeclampsia was too advanced, and the doctors had to act fast.

Baye was delivered via emergency C-section November 21. She weighed 1 pound 12 ounces, and she was 11 inches long. She was so tiny, but so beautiful. The next three and a half months were spent in the NICU. My little baby lived in an incubator with tubes coming from every part of her body. It broke my heart, but little did I know that was just the beginning.

Three days following her birth, one of the nurses told me that Baye was losing blood and they wanted to do a routine cranial ultrasound to rule out any brain bleeds that preemies sometimes get. They told me to not think much about it, so I didn't. Looking back I realize that when someone tells you not to think about something, you probably should.

When I came to the NICU later that day, one of the nurses told me that the attending physician wanted to speak with me. My heart fell to the floor. I knew something was wrong when the doctor sat down with a piece of paper and a pen. She began drawing something and said that Baye had Schizencephaly; she might as well have been speaking a foreign language. She drew a picture of a brain missing a part. She explained to me that Baye's brain did not develop like a normal brain. I don't really remember what else she said after that, I just walked over to Baye's incubator and placed my hand in it. I put my pinky finger in her little hand and I prayed for the Lord to help me understand why this had happened.

Baye's doctors did not have much to say about Schizencephaly. During the entire three and a half months she was in the NICU, the only answers I got were from the research I had done online. I was told by a neurosurgeon to not expect much out of Baye, because she may be like a vegetable for the rest of her life. It was then that I took a step back and became determined to help my daughter accomplish things the doctors said was impossible.

When Baye was four months old, she developed Hydrocephalus and had a shunt placed to drain the fluid. Hydrocephalus (water on the brain) is a medical condition in which there is an abnormal accumulation of cerebrospinal fluid in the ventricles (cavities) of the brain.

Baye is legally blind, but because of her age, we are not sure how bad her eyes are. We do know that she has small optic nerves, and that is typical for children with Schizencephaly. It means there is no cortical blindness, but the nerve that takes the visual picture back to the brain is damaged, causing poor vision.

She also has suffered from subclinical seizures while in the NICU. They stopped right before she was discharged, but later diagnosed with Tonic-Clinic seizures, infantile spasms, and partial and complex seizures. Baye is on five seizure medications, and has recently started Sabril, a drug that is not commonly used because it is a new experimental drug. We will not continue that one for too long since the effects do cause complete blindness after prolonged use.

Baye is behind developmentally. She is now 15 months old and does not reach for toys, make baby sounds, or have any head or body control. She is currently in physical and occupational therapy to help her development.

I say that Baye does not do these things, but she actually does so much more. She has big blue eyes that love to watch Elmo and Mickey. She has strong little hands that love to hold her mommy's necklace, the cutest laugh, the most beautiful smile in the world, and she is the best little snuggle buddy. Baye has a way of touching people, and everyone that sees her falls in love.

Baye is still very young, and I know we have a long way to go, but

TRICIA DENNIS and STEPHANIE ZIEMANN

Gracelyn

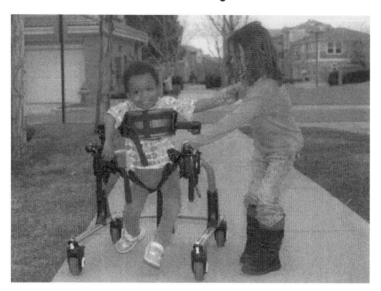

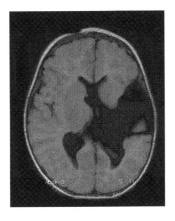

Back in the summer of 2009, my husband, Joshua, and I were contemplating adoption and went to an informative meeting about the subject. We talked about what we could handle when moving forward with adoption, and knew that taking special needs situation would be on a case-by-case basis.

So many different situations were presented with the adoption process that it became overwhelming, and we decided to sign on with a consultant to help us throughout the process. We experienced a series of emotional challenges after multiple failed placements. Then one day, Joshua and I received a call that an expecting mother from Utah wanted us to be the adopting parents of her child, and that she wanted us to be there for the birth. The consultant warned us that the child was expected to have some sort of disability, but we didn't mind, we were happy to have been finally chosen.

As soon as Joshua got off work, we jumped in the car and headed for Utah. We made one stop to drop off our oldest daughter at her grandparents, and then we hurried as fast as we could to make it in time for the birth, but not fast enough. We had missed the birth by three hours.

We met with the birth mother and it went great. Then we went over to the nursery and held our daughter for the first time. We even got to give our little girl her first bath and spend that night in the hospital with her. The adoption papers were signed the next day, and Gracelyn was ours. Over the next few months, Joshua and I completed the steps to finalize our daughter's adoption.

Gracelyn was doing very well in the beginning and showed no signs of having a disability. She wasn't rolling over at four months old, and we figured she was just developing at her own pace; but she still wasn't rolling around or moving much at six months old, her right arm was very tight, and her hand staid in a fist. We grew concerned and told the pediatrician we wanted to take Gracelyn to a neurologist, he agreed.

Her neurologist's initial assumption was that she had Cerebral Palsy, and ordered a MRI to confirm his diagnosis. The results showed that she had Schizencephaly. We started treating the condition right away with physical and occupational therapy, and were told not to expect a lot of progress.

Joshua and I knew that we would do whatever it took to give Gracelyn the best in life. We worked hard, but to be truthful, we saw little or no change in our sweet Gracelyn. That caused me to have many sleepless, tear-filled nights. There were times that I wouldn't even get the mail because the thought of another medical bill made me physically ill. But I had to hold myself together so that our four year old would not ask why I was crying.

In May 2012, we made the choice to move to Colorado for several reasons. One being the Children's Hospital, and the other was my family. We moved in with my parents while we were transitioning, and Gracelyn started to make incredible improvements. In July 2012, our baby girl went from laying flat on her back, to sitting up without any help. Then several weeks later, she started Army crawling. Her growth was partially due to a long lost friend; my parents' dog.

We were also pleased with our decision to move to Utah because Gracelyn was finally receiving care from doctors who actually believed in our princess. And when paired with the help of her therapists, she started to make even greater strides in her motor and verbal skills.

One day, Gracelyn lifted her leg and tried to take a step. I started to do tons of research to find the best option for walkers, and by the end of November we had one being submitted to insurance. While waiting on that, one of the programs we were participating in loaned us a walker to get her accustomed to walking with assistance. Once again she was breaking expectations and gaining skills that most people would have never thought she'd accomplish.

Gracelyn got her first Botox injection in her right arm mid-December, and what a difference it has made. She can now lift it without the aid of her left arm. One of the hardest parts throughout this journey is never truly getting a break from what seems like endless appointments, and being on constant guard for unexpected illnesses and seizures.

It still amazes me how far our children can go when they are given the opportunity and the fact that most doctors believe there is no hope for these kids. I also believe that had we not adopted Gracelyn, we would have never been blessed to have a relationship with a birth mom that changed our level of love. Raising her is teaching us that everything we will face down the road is worth the fight. We can honestly say that without our oldest daughter and Gracelyn, our "Angel with a Broken Wing", we may have never understood the real meaning of unconditional love.

TRICIA DENNIS and STEPHANIE ZIEMANN

ABOUT THE AUTHOR'S

Tricia Dennis

Tricia began her career as an early intervention student with Hadley School for the Blind, and moved forward into public speaking and avocation after the birth of her second son, Noah.

In 2002, she won second place in a Florida State writing contest for her story, My Biggest Dream. A short story depicting the life of what she wished for her son and the reality of what life was truly like. In 2008, Tricia left her real estate career and began Noah's Cart, That same year, her story was submitted to Nancy Grace, and Tricia was featured as a finalist for an Extraordinary Parent Contest.

Tricia's life mission is to make a difference and spread awareness on this disorder. She and Noah travel all over speaking about in-utero stroke and the complications that come with Noah's disorder.

Stephanie Ziemann

Stephanie Ziemann is the mother of Ada-Lily, a director of Noah's Cart, and is committed to raising awareness and becoming an advocate for not only her daughter, but all families touched by Schizencephaly. Stephanie is looking to give a voice to this disorder, as well as enlightening professionals that do not have enough experience with Schizencephaly so that they can better assess and treat their patients with more accurate and hopeful outcomes. She is currently working with Tricia Dennis to raise awareness and change the face of Schizencephaly.

TRICIA DENNIS and STEPHANIE ZIEMANN

We would like to give a special thank you to our friend, Sara. Without you, we would be all over the page.

Websites

www.noahscart.org

www.facebook.com/SchizencephalyAwarenessNoahDennis

www.islanddolphincare.org

www.cmvfoundation.org

Made in the USA
Columbia, SC
10 May 2020